THE WORSHIP BOOK

edited by Sarah James

The Worship Book
edited by Sarah James

Published by MU enterprises Ltd
Mary Sumner House
24 Tufton Street
London SW1P 3RB
0171 222 5533

ISBN 0 85943 058 8

Printed and Bound by Bourne Press Limited, Bournemouth

ACKNOWLEDGEMENTS

Grateful acknowledgment must be made of the work done by Canon Rachel Stowe and the group of people (Rosemary Peirce, Felicity Randall and her husband Ian, Christine McMullen, and Lynda Howells) who researched and gathered much of the material for this book over several months, and to all the members of the Mothers' Union who completed the questionnaire about the scope of the book, made suggestions and contributed prayers.

Special thanks are due to Christine Eames, the World Wide President and to Rosalind Smith, Joan Stannard, Dorothy Knights, the Venerable Mark Dalby, the Central Chaplain of the Mothers' Union the Right Revd. Frank Sargeant and the Right Revd. Colin Buchanan who have all given me much helpful criticism.

Not all the contributions or all the criticism have been incorporated, so the faults and shortcomings are mine. I apologise for mistakes made especially in the attribution of copyright; for prayers this is always a delicate matter: words and sources are heard and appreciated but only recalled and written down later, not always accurately. Some prayers have been culled from other collections, and although the original source has been pursued wherever possible, it is hard to be confident that credit has been given correctly: the Mothers' Union will be pleased to receive amendments.

I must also thank the staff at Mary Sumner House for the help they have given to me and to the earlier working group: Janet Bailey, Roger Cozens, Gill England, Diana Murrie, Angela Ridler and Jenny Rooke have each made a contribution to the process, and the Mothers' Union is grateful to them.

Rochester

Sarah A. L. James   December 1994

PART I ~ Practicalities

PART II ~ Services you could use

PARTS III ~ Resources

PART I

Practicalities

WHY HAVE A MOTHERS' UNION WORSHIP BOOK?

· The Worship Book has been produced in response to many requests from all parts of the Mothers' Union to provide additional material to augment the forms of service in the *Mothers' Union Service Book*. The "blue book", as it is affectionately called, (to differentiate it from the previous red *Mothers' Union Service Book* (1948) or the even older brown book), was produced (in 1976) to reflect the outcome of *New Dimensions* and the changes made to the Constitution and in particular the Objects. At the time it began to be used, church congregations in Britain and Ireland and other provinces of the Anglican Communion were still only just getting used to new texts that would be developed as alternatives to the Book of Common Prayer.

Since then Anglican worship has continued to develop and many of the texts of the 1970's feel dated and often unsatisfactory; some of the language seems banal or clumsy, much of it is exclusive, not only in terms of gender but also in matters of age and culture. The 1974 Mothers' Union Prayer had often been criticised by people who felt excluded because they were unmarried, or no longer married, so the prayer was amended in March 1994. The society has become much more flexible in adopting terminology appropriate to local needs, e.g. chairman for president, branch leader for enrolling member, worldwide in place of overseas. Departmental arrangements vary from province to province and diocese to diocese. There is a growth in the number of members who are men.

It is time to provide material for worship that reflects these changes; time not to abolish what has served the society well and is much loved, but to provide alternatives. The "blue book" was intended to replace previous books, not least because the Constitution and the Mothers' Union Prayer had been changed; this book is intended to be complementary - to be used alongside the "blue book", and its companion the red *Mothers' Union Prayer Book,* and alongside the *Anthology of Public Prayer (1989).* For that reason it does not itself include a full collection of prayers.

THE SCOPE OF THIS BOOK
GETTING STARTED

This book will not solve everybody's problems; it may help people to solve them themselves. It asks as many questions as it gives answers; it recommends a number of resources, but most people who are expected to arrange or lead worship already have their own favourites, or have access to people or books that can help. In Part I, chapter 1 explains how to use the book and the material it contains while chapter 2 considers how to build a service, reminds leaders of some of the practical considerations in leading worship, and gives a checklist that can ensure the whole service is balanced. Chapter 3 gives some reminders about the content and techniques of leading prayers and chapter 4 looks at the important question of permission to use copyright material. Chapter 5 deals at some length with pram and parent-and-toddler services and explains why it has not been thought appropriate to include material specifically for this type of worship. These are general chapters which should really be read before turning to the later pages.

Chapter 6 provides four service outlines, trying to help people identify a suitable shape for their worship, and an outline for a day of prayer or vigil.

FORMS OF SERVICE

Part II includes a number of forms of service which Mothers' Union leaders and members have asked for in recent years. It is possible that one of them will be exactly what you, your branch, and your incumbent are looking for; it is much more likely that you will want to modify the material, omitting some of it and borrowing from other parts of this book or elsewhere: it is important that you do so, because in worship it is wise to be careful to use words that are appropriate for the people and the occasion.

The chapters in this section are arranged more or less in line with the five Objects of the Mothers' Union. So chapter 7 concentrates on MARRIAGE with a Marriage Celebration service which could be used for a couple to renew their marriage, or celebrate an anniversary, or as the basis of a deanery or diocesan festival.... Chapter 8 focuses on FAMILY LIFE and CHILDREN, and their faith: it contains a Mothering Sunday service and some prayers for Mothering Sunday.

Family life also features in the various forms of prayers given in chapter 9. Here you can find new forms for branch and committee MEETINGS, for morning, mid-day and afternoon or evening use; the three forms for mid-day prayers are each different: one is very short for use in committee meetings, one concentrates on the worldwide wave of prayer and the other (from *Celebrating Common Prayer)* has different aspects of family life as its focus.

Chapter 10 contains three forms of particular use to prayer groups: an outline which allows for considerable periods of silence, and so is particularly appropriate for use by a small (or smaller) group, a litany of prayer celebrating women of faith throughout the ages, and an outline of a seasonal (or thematic) nature which needs to be amplified by material from the collection of relevant Bible references and the extensive selection of relevant prayers and collects from around the world, which can be found in Part III of this book. Of course the leader can also include other prayers and readings e.g. from the Mothers' Union *Anthology of Public Prayer*.

In chapter 11 can be found forms for admission (enrolment of new members), commissioning of officers, dedication of a new branch, and a service for the closure of a group or branch. It also includes the service of re-affirmation of baptism and membership promises which arose out of the *I believe and trust* initiative.

Chapter 12 is concerned with times of special need and includes a service of healing from Iona. Aspects of adversity in family life are included both here and in chapters 8 and 9.

FURTHER RESOURCES

Part III consists of a variety of resources: in chapter 13 there is a number of words of introduction to the Lord's Prayer and of responses which can be used in intercessory litanies; also provided are the texts of several items that recur thoughout the book. In order to save repetition in the main text the Mothers' Union Prayer, the Grace, the Lord's Prayer in both traditional and modern forms have been printed on the inside and back cover for easy access. In chapter 13 there is also a list of hymns and songs about marriage and family life, and a modest collection of suggested Bible readings and prayers on the themes and seasons, for use particularly with the "Round the Year" outline in chapter 10.

Chapter 14 provides a list of publications which can provide additional material for the worship leader and some useful addresses; inevitably some of these will become out of date, but much of the material is "standard" and fairly timeless: publications which are out of print may possibly be borrowed from clergy or other lay leaders.

THE WORDS WE USE

The prayers are primarily for public, Mothers' Union, occasions, but are also suitable for private or other church use. It has been hard to make a selection as members composed or suggested many prayers which could have been included: however this book, as stated at the beginning, is intended to complement and run alongside other Mothers' Union prayer and service books, so the material has been tightly controlled.

As individual members of the Mothers' Union we live in very varied situations, and when we meet we each bring a wealth of experience; gathering the different strands together in our prayers makes for great richness in worship. Sharing the leadership, and taking time to prepare the service, will both allow this richness to find expression and also deepen the prayer life of all the members.

When we come to pray we are often aware of the size and enormity of the problems in the world. We may feel paralysed by them, or depressed by guilt because we are doing nothing about them - or we may want to press for changes in a frenzy of activity; we need to recognise and acknowledge these feelings, and use words to express them.

If we use prayers that say we are poor when we are living in the lap of luxury, our words may appear hypocritical. Yet even if we are privileged in a material sense, we can admit we are each diminished and wounded because of the poverty and injustice that affects others, whether close to us or further afield. As members of a worldwide organisation we recognise our mutual inter-dependence and welcome our relationships with each other.

As we pray we offer ourselves, expecting to be shaped or changed by the gospel, both as individuals and as communities. Our prayers will be more "real" if we appreciate the differences in our situations, and then pray for change, working with love, honesty and commitment for the benefit of everybody. Our prayers put us in God's hands, nourish our commitment, and help us see His vision of a different kind of world.

ANGLICAN WORSHIP ...

As a voluntary society within the Anglican communion, the Mothers' Union naturally tends to use Anglican patterns of prayer and worship. Even when extempore prayer is included the prayers are likely to be Biblically based, to include the Lord's Prayer and to end with the Grace.

This helps everyone present to feel at ease and, because they are free from anxiety, to be able to lift their hearts to God. When putting together a form of worship, whether for a major service in a church, or a small group of people meeting for prayer in someone's house, it is important to be deliberate in choosing what to put in and what to omit.

The elements that are likely to be found in satisfactory services are:

- a verse or verses from the Bible, especially from the New Testament; this may be as a reading, or in the form of canticles, psalms, chants (e.g. Taize).

- responsorial material, either well-known (e.g. Lord in your mercy, Hear our prayer) or with instruction (e.g. we're going to use a new response today: when I say "Heavenly Father" please will you reply "Hear your children's prayer". Let's just try that before we start: "Heavenly.....").

- prayers in the form of collects, i.e. addressing God (e.g. "Almighty God"), describing him (e.g. "who gave marriage to be a source of blessing..."), asking for something (e.g. "Pour out upon us..."), looking for a result (e.g. "that we may truly love and serve....") ending with an ascription (e.g. "through Jesus Christ our Lord") and "Amen".

- the Lord's Prayer in traditional or modern form.

- a recognisable structure, in shape and content, even when new and varied material (readings, music, action, or symbols) is introduced.

.... SUITABLE FOR ALL

Within these conventions there is still a great deal of room for personal choice by whoever is putting together the service, and a number of questions it is appropriate to ask:

- who is likely to be there, and what are their likely needs?

- what is the purpose of the service? Apart from the essential aim of giving glory to God, is the service intended to start a new stage in life (e.g. commissioning or admission service), or to celebrate something (e.g. family life or marriage or the millenium), or is it part of the regular weekly or monthly diet of a group's worship? Or is it a time of dedication for a working committee, asking for God's help in the business to be done?

- in the light of the answers to these questions, do we want the service to have a specific theme, or should it focus on the season of the Church's year, or a saint's day?

- what is the appropriate use of silence for these people and on this occasion?

- is there any particular material it would be helpful to include such as poetry or other non-Biblical readings, drama, liturgical dance, dialogue or a talk?

- will each person have a copy of the book or service? Would it be helpful to duplicate a paper for each person? (If so care must be taken to observe the laws of copyright *(see chapter 4)*. Do people need hymn or song books?

- what versions of the reading(s) would be best? Consider splitting a reading between different voices or using the Dramatised Bible (see resources).

❖   what provision is made in the service for the traditional elements of
      Adoration and Praise of God
      Confession of our wrongdoing
      Thanksgiving for God's blessings
      Supplication for others and ourselves?

❖   in a service with music do the styles complement or compete? If
      there are hymns and songs are they varied in key, verse shape,
      mood and style?

❖   the end and the beginning need special care. Shall we start with
      words of welcome or an explanation? End with the grace or a
      blessing (in "us" form if no priest is present), or in some other way?

❖   is it advisable to specify when people should stand, sit or kneel?
      Would doing so help people to feel at ease?

❖   is there scope for inter-active worship?

... WORSHIPPING TOGETHER

With an eye to the future it is worthwhile encouraging different people to
use their talents in the worship: reading the Bible or the collect for the day,
putting together the prayers (and / or leading them), choosing hymns or
songs and leading the singing or playing the piano, giving out books or
sheets and tidying them away afterwards, setting out the room, arranging
flowers, lighting a candle, or finding a picture on the theme, are all ways in
which people can contribute. Unless people are very confident they should
always be asked at least the day before, to give them time to prepare
properly.

It is important to see that every act of worship is balanced in itself, and
just as the prayer should include something from each of the A-C-T-S
elements (see above), so the contents of the readings from the Bible or

elsewhere should be balanced, but care must be taken to avoid putting too much into any one service: over a period one hopes to cover the whole spectrum of Christian, Mothers' Union and personal life but there is always next time! Each service needs to be selective, and each service needs a focus. Planning a term or a year's worship is as important as planning the rest of the programme; usually the two are inter-dependent.

THEMES

By narrowing the focus the prayer can be more specific and people may find the worship has a greater depth. There are different approaches:

a   build the worship round the activity of the group; e.g. the topic for the meeting, a recent visit, or the forthcoming outreach event.

b   follow the lectionary theme from the previous Sunday's worship; e.g. "The Way, the Truth, the Life" or "The Fruits of the Spirit".

c   focus on some part of parish or diocesan life; e.g. Baptism, Confirmation or Marriage Preparation, Stewardship, or Mission and Unity.

d   pick up on the season: celebrate Spring, or Holidays.

e   concentrate on one aspect of Mothers' Union life, or one of the Objects; e.g. Action and Outreach, Marriage, Families in Adversity, or the Worldwide Fellowship.

THE BIBLE

When we are enrolled we promise to plan our lives to include Bible Reading, but sometimes this becomes a struggle and we need encouragement and new inspiration to keep this promise; hearing the Bible read aloud, perhaps in a slighty unusual way, can be really helpful.

The version and the method of presentation should be chosen carefully: short readings, read quite slowly and with time for silent reflection can be particularly helpful. Longer readings can be read by several voices, perhaps using the "Dramatised Bible", or writing your own script from the Bible; verses on a theme (e.g.The Good Shepherd, or Mary, Mother of Our Lord, or the Kingdom) from different parts of the Bible can be put together with great effect, especially with pauses, or taped music between each verse. A reading followed by a prayer based on the reading (e.g. from "Bible Praying") can provide a neat item in a time of worship. The psalms should not be overlooked.

MUSIC

Once upon a time most branch meetings had at least one hymn, often accompanied by an out of tune piano, as part of the opening prayers; as fewer members are willing or able to play the piano this custom has fallen off, but now with Iona songs and Taize chants, and the availability of guitars and flutes, cassette tapes and keyboards, music is coming back into meetings. Many modern worship songs can be sung unaccompanied, and both music and words are quickly learnt, either line by line, or from an overhead projector or songsheet, and are as appropriate for a service in church as for a meeting in a hall or house.

SILENCE

Most Christians are busy people and the effort required to get to a meeting or service can be considerable, whether one has small children, voluntary or paid responsibilities, or reduced health or mobility. If people are to continue to make the effort they need to find the time with others rewarding; they need to find space for themselves, stimulation and interest, to experience something of God and to enjoy fellowship with others.

Silence can allow both space and a shared experience of God, but people need to know where they are, and what is happening. It's easy to waste precious silence by being anxious: "What am I meant to be doing /

thinking?", "How long have I got?", or even "Has the leader lost her place / nodded off?" So "a minute's silence" should be just that, timed for sixty seconds. It's unfair to say "two minutes' silence" and make it five minutes or thirty seconds. People get into the way of silence, whether it comes in the intercessions in church on Sunday, or in a small group meeting for prayer, and will gradually come to appreciate longer periods, but it is probably wise to start with a shorter time. The leader, if alert, can usually spot when people begin almost imperceptibly to fidget, lifting their heads or moving their feet, and can then gently bring it to an end, perhaps with a recognised formula e.g. "Lord in your mercy, hear our prayer".

Silence in worship can provide space for people to meet, hear and respond to the Spirit of God.

CHECKLIST

1   Does the worship give honour to God and serve to build up his people?

2   Do the prayers address God rather than the people?

3   Is there a balance between prayer, Bible or other reading, and movement? Is there enough or too much of each? Is the prayer a balanced mixture of praise, penitence, and petition?

4   Is it clear what is expected of the people at every stage? What about the balance of standing, sitting and kneeling?

5   Is there enough time for reflection and silence?

6   Do the different parts of the service follow in a logical sequence, each leading into the next? Is the mix right between longer and shorter items?

7   Are there enough different participants, or too many?

8   Does the service move to a climax, and is there then an anti-climax, or a gentle winding-down?

9   What is the predominant mood of the worship and is it appropriate?

10   If there is music is it used to help the worship? Is it balanced in style and content, and appropriately placed in the whole?

11   If there is an element of entertainment is it excessive?

12   Is the language of the prayers and readings appropriate, especially if there are children or newcomers present, or single people and widows (i.e. without jargon, inclusive and sensitive)?

13   Is there a reasonable balance between novelty and what is familiar?

14   Do all the leaders, including the clergy, know what is expected of them, and when?

15   If there is a collection who will take it and where will it go?

16   If there is an expected time length for the service (tacit or declared), will the chosen material fit the expectations?

17   Does the whole service have a definite beginning and end?

It is a great honour to be asked to lead worship or lead the prayers, and even if we feel unworthy to do so we should accept the privilege as a way of serving our friends as well as serving God. Advance preparation and prayer (for the task, for the other people and for oneself), will equip us for the time we shall spend together before God.

When praying in public it is easy to feel you are not really praying yourself; there is no need to be anxious about this - your devotion has gone into the preparation and you are now involved in helping others to pray.

Prayers are an important part of any occasion, sometimes giving everything else an extra dimension. Even people new to the Church respect their significance. There may be people present who have previously only heard public prayers in church or at school and who may find informal prayers in modern language strange: keep the grammar simple.

BEFORE YOU START

There are a number of decisions to be made before you start; you may have no choice about some of them because of the nature of the occasion, the people who will be there, or the usual custom of the group. If you are uncertain consult whoever asked you to lead the prayers. You will need to consider:

❖   whether to follow an accepted format, or try some new idea, or include different things in the usual pattern of prayer

❖   what material has to be included, and what else would make it balanced

❖   is the style to be formal or informal?

❖   should everything be addressed to God, or should biddings (instructions to the people) be used to introduce each prayer?

❖   if you prefer "Thee and Thou" or "You", or a mixture

- which version of the Lord's Prayer to use (chapter 13. 1 and p176)
- what use will be made of silence, extempore prayer, of well-known collects or a litany
- should people sit or stand or kneel? Should you stand and the others sit or kneel? Should you face them or be among them?
- how you are going to start, and end
- if there is anything else that could help people be at ease, and feel that they are indeed praying
- although most meetings start with prayer, whether an epilogue at the end would be appropriate

PRACTICAL POINTS

- It is wise to have the words of the Lord's Prayer in front of you; when you are leader it is very easy to make a conspicuous mistake.
- Modern prayers with unfamiliar words should be read more slowly than, for instance, familiar collects; people need time to make the words their own.
- Be audible: without shouting, speak as if to the person in the far corner of the room or church; this may not feel devout, but is essential for the other people.
- If there is a hymn join in and so loosen your voice; breathe out thoroughly two or three times before you start, to relax yourself and provide a good supply of oxygen.
- Wait until everyone is quiet before you start.
- Be dignified: prayer should never be hurried; it is better to say less, but slowly; allow space between different topics.
- Avoid some "triggers": if you say "Let us pray" in an Anglican church the congregation may well drop to their knees. In the same way the words "in Jesus's name", or dropping your voice at the end of the sentence will almost always provoke an "Amen".

❖   Try to have a logical order to your prayers e.g. start with God, then
       proceed through the world and/or the Church and the Mothers'
       Union, any special interest or activity, ending with prayers for
       individuals.

❖   If you want to use several books have them ready, in the correct
       order, on a table or spare chair in front of you. Try to avoid having
       to turn too many pages; numbered markers in each place and a
       small pencil mark in the margin will help you find the prayers you
       want at the right moment.

❖   Or you can write the prayers in a notebook or on cards (pieces of
       paper may tremble if you are nervous) and in this way gradually
       build up your own collection of useful prayers. Do not hesitate to
       alter anything which is inappropriate to the occasion.

PRAYERS AT A MEETING

Usually prayers at a meeting consist of a brief act of praise and
thanksgiving followed by prayers for the work of the meeting; they can
include prayers for vision and wisdom, for courage and humility to know
God's will and pursue it. Often absent members are remembered in prayer.

In Mothers' Union day-time meetings it is usual at noon to pray for
members round the world, using the Wave of Prayer calendar (printed
each quarter in *Home & Family*).

It is important that everyone knows what is expected of them: give out
page or hymn numbers clearly. If people are to say the Mothers' Union
Prayer give them time to find the words (in a Service or Worship Book, on
a card or in their diary) before the prayer time starts.

The end is as important as the beginning. You can end with the Grace (see
inside back cover) introduced by such words as "To close our meeting/ to
end our time together, let's (join hands and) say the Grace.. " Whatever

words are used the leader should indicate when she has finished, so that people can get up or start talking.

Prayer is a two-way movement; as we tune in to God he transmits his grace and power to us and through us to other people. There will be times when our prayers will be inspired beyond the preparation we have done; as leaders we shall often find we have received immeasurably more than we have given. And sometimes we will know the joy of realising in a new way the presence of Jesus Christ "in the midst of us".

Anybody considering printing or photocopying service sheets or using an overhead projector (OHP) to provide words for worship needs to be aware of the law of copyright.

Basically it is the right of authors, composers and publishers to receive a fee each time their material is duplicated, in lieu of the money they would have received if the organiser had bought a copy of the original (book or sheet, words and music) for every worshipper. In general, short extracts, less than twenty lines or 250 words can be used from prose works or poems without permission, and without payment of a fee, but the source and author should always be acknowledged. Works remain in copyright until 31st December after the fiftieth anniversary of the death of the author, translator, composer or arranger.

PHOTOCOPYING

The rules about the photocopying of texts are much more restrictive than for handwriting or typing / word-processing; changes to the texts require different and separate permission; modern adapted versions of old texts (e.g. in *Hymns for Today's Church*) require copyright permission from the adaptor.

BIBLE PASSAGES

Different practical arrangements exist for the many possible sources of the songs, hymns, prayers and readings that you are likely to want to use: *The Authorised Version of the Bible* and *the Book of Common Prayer* are both Crown property and, although they are old, are still in copyright; application to reproduce substantial passages should be made to Cambridge University Press: permission is usually freely given, but acknowledgement must be made.

Many publishers allow verses of the Bible to be copied up to a certain maximum (*Good News Bible / Today's English Version:* 250 verses, *Jerusalem Bible / New Jerusalem Bible,* and the *Revised Standard Version*

/ *New Revised Standard Version:* 500 verses, *New International Version:* 1,000 verses) without application.

CHURCH OF ENGLAND TEXTS

Texts from the *Alternative Service Book 1980* and its separate booklets, along with *Lent, Holy Week, Easter: Services and Prayers* and *The Promise of His Glory* are the property of The Central Board of Finance of the Church of England; they may be reproduced for non-commercial one-time use by Anglican churches, as long as the name of the church, cathedral or institution, is shown and the date of the service. See *Liturgical Texts for Local Use 1994*, the useful booklet issued by the Central Board of Finance of the General Synod of the Church of England (obtainable for 75p from Church House Publishing, Great Smith Street, London SW1P 3NZ and religious bookshops).

OTHER CHURCHES

For texts of the Church in Wales, Episcopal Church of Scotland, the Church of Ireland, churches of other provinces in the Anglican Communion or in other denominations, application should be made to the relevant central administrative office.

HYMNS AND WORSHIP SONGS

It is usually possible to trace the copyright owner of hymns and songs through the *Acknowledgements* page of the source book; where no source is shown there, or immediately after the item in the book, it is best to write to the publisher. Very often no charge will be made for one-time use in worship, though some publishers impose a handling charge for waiving the copyright fee! Publishers in the U.S.A. require their fees to be paid in dollars.

LICENCE SCHEMES

Many churches now subscribe to one of the inclusive copyright licensing schemes which allow material from a variety of sources to be copied, with a record kept of items used, for an annual fee. If your church, or cathedral, has such a licence, it should include Mothers' Union services. It is not at present (1994) possible for an individual to take out a licence.

Individual publishers often have their own conditions under which material may be copied; many of them allow free reproduction as long as written permission is sought in advance (or sometimes within seven days of use). Stainer & Bell, (Victoria House, 23 Gruneisen Road, Finchley, London N3 1DZ) have published *The Churches' Copyright Directory* which shows these publishers, and the requirements of most other publishers; it also lists the copyright administrators of most of the hymns and songs in the major hymn and song books in use in churches in the United Kingdom.

MOTHERS' UNION MATERIAL

Mothers' Union material may be reproduced by the Mothers' Union as long as acknowledgement is made of its source; other organisations or individuals should write for permission to The Mothers' Union, Mary Sumner House, 24 Tufton Street, London SW1P 3RB.

Each Pram Service is an individual and unique event, which depends on many variable factors for its form and content, especially

WHY?	the aim / purpose of having a pram service
WHO?	the people who may want to come - children's ages, adults' level of Christian experience and commitment
WHO?	the people who are available as leaders, whether clergy or lay
WHERE?	the building - church or hall
WHEN?	the time - mid-morning, just before lunch, or afternoon
HOW?	the usual worship style of the parish

Pram services usually evolve and develop, and it is important that they should do so appropriately as people and conditions change. The original group of children and mothers will grow older and more experienced; some will move away; some will bring in friends and neighbours; some will continue to come with a second (or third) child. A group that has many very young children one year may have predominantly three year olds two years later, or they may all have moved on and the group be back to babies. Sometimes there may be several fathers, at other times some child minders or grannies.

LEADERSHIP

The leadership will probably change, particularly if the service is led, or partly led, by some of the parents. As people come and go so will their strengths - their skills and abilities and interests. As time goes by leaders gain confidence, and can branch out and try more ambitious things; on the other hand it is wise to meet the expectations of those who come by using an accepted pattern each time, even if within that pattern there may be considerable variety of content.

INDIVIDUALITY

It would not be appropriate to give forms of service in this book, as that would appear to prescribe the "right" way of doing things: the only right way is the way that gives glory to God and suits the individuals taking part. No set service can allow for changing people and circumstances. There are many good ideas and suggestions in *Let's have a pram service* (published by the Mothers' Union) together with a useful checklist of things to remember, and in the *Together* magazine and books (published by Church House Publishing), as well as many books from other religious publishers.

SHORT AND SIMPLE

A golden rule is to keep the act of worship short, simple and unhurried. Twenty minutes is probably long enough, unless there is some activity included which means people moving round the building (e.g. lighting birthday candles), in which case an extra two or three minutes may be needed. Use simple everyday words: welcome people as you might welcome them to your home; tell the story and say prayers in your own words; try not to use a script.

SHAPE AND CONTENT

A common shape for a pram service is

welcome - song - story - song - prayer -song - goodbye

Any part of it may include actions for people to do. It is a good idea for the first song to be a gathering / joining song, the second one to relate back to the story, and the third song be a celebrating, or going-out song. It is helpful if there is someone who can play the piano or keyboard, or a guitar, but cassette tapes (e.g. *Junior Praise, Come & Praise*, or the tape produced by Eunice Norwood of London Diocese MU) are nearly as good, as long as the building is not too large.

The story can be a story, or part of one, from the Bible, or elsewhere (e.g. Roger Hargreaves' *Mister Men* or *Little Miss* books), or one that you have made up. On the other hand the "story" may be an activity. The words for the songs should either be learnt by heart, line by line, or displayed on an overhead projector or very large sheet of paper; people with small children cannot easily manage songsheets, especially if they want to clap or do actions with their hands as well. The prayer can include thanksgiving as well as asking, but the words must be said slowly and clearly and the concepts kept simple. This is an example:

> Dear Father God,
> bless our families;
> in them may we know your love for us
> and show our love for you,
> through Jesus Christ, our Lord. **Amen.**
> *(from Revd David Yabbacombe, Rector of Cheadle with Freehay)*

SITE AND CONTEXT

The service can be held in any part of the church - in the chancel, around the font, in a side chapel, or even the belfry or vestry, if there is no suitable space in the nave. Use the space appropriately, e.g. if you want to talk about a baby being baptized gather round the font.

Thought needs to be given to the whole context in which the pram service is held: in some places the service is part of a weekly provision for parents and small children; in others it may happen three or six times a year, in which case more work needs to be done to attract people to come. In either case publicity can be through local clinics, hospital or health visitors, the library, shop windows, or nursery schools as well as through the Church congregation. Parents bringing children to baptism at the church should certainly be encouraged to come as a way of fulfilling their promise to bring the child up in the faith.

Wherever possible refreshments should be available before or after the service and it is helpful if the vicar or rector and other parish staff can be there to talk to people and get to know them.

*1: Suitable for **A BRANCH, DEANERY, DIOCESAN or OTHER SERVICE,** in church, hall or house, without Holy Communion*

THE PREPARATION
Welcome
Hymn, Psalm or Song
Confession *(with or without Absolution)*

THE MINISTRY OF THE WORD
Reading
Silence
Hymn, Psalm, Canticle or Scriptural Song
Reading
Sermon or Talk
Creed or Affirmation of Faith

THE ACTION *as appropriate*
Baptism, Admission, Commissioning or Presentation
Welcome of specific people; demonstration or appeal.

THE PRAYERS
Intercessions and Thanksgivings
The Lord's Prayer
The Mothers' Union Prayer

THE CONCLUSION
Hymn or Song *(for collection)*
Offertory Prayer
Blessing, Grace and / or Dismissal

2: *Suitable for* **A BRANCH, DEANERY or DIOCESAN SERVICE**
in church, with Holy Communion

THE PREPARATION
Welcome
Hymn, Psalm or Song
Confession and Absolution

THE MINISTRY OF THE WORD
Reading (*followed by silence)*
Hymn, Psalm, Canticle or Scriptural Song
Gospel Reading
Sermon or Talk
Creed

THE PRAYERS
Intercessions and Thanksgivings
(*including* The Mothers' Union Prayer)
The Peace
Hymn or Song *(for collection)*
The Eucharistic Prayer
The Lord's Prayer

THE COMMUNION
Post-Communion Prayer *(see chapter 11.1 - Commissioning)*

THE CONCLUSION
Blessing and / or Dismissal
Final Hymn or Song

3: *Suitable for a* **PRAISE & PRAYER SERVICE**

THE PREPARATION
Welcome
Hymn or Song of Praise
Prayer of Thanksgiving
Prayer of Penitence
Reflective Song(s) or Chants

THE MINISTRY OF THE WORD
Reading
Silence
Hymn, Psalm, Chant (e.g. Taize) or Scriptural Song
Talk or Drama
Response: an Affirmation of Faith, Worship Song(s),
or Prayer of Personal Commitment

THE PRAYERS
Intercessions and Thanksgivings
The Lord's Prayer
Hymn or Song

THE CONCLUSION
Final Hymn or Song
Blessing, Grace and / or Dismissal

4: *Suitable for **A PRAM OR TODDLER SERVICE***

THE PREPARATION
Welcome
Song

THE MINISTRY OF THE WORD
Story
Song

THE PRAYER
Prayer
The Lord's Prayer

THE CONCLUSION
Song
Good-byes

5: *Suitable for* **A DAY OF PRAYER or VIGIL**

The time available could be divided into hour sessions, with two slots of twenty-five minutes of active prayer and worship in each session. People should be asked, in advance, to arrive as quietly as possible in the first five minutes of the hour and to leave in the last five minutes of the hour, (or, if essential, at the half-hour mid-point).

	Suggested timing
Introduction of the theme of the next half-hour, and how it is to be spent	**2 mins**
Opening prayer a Collect, or a prayer to settle people and gather their attention	**2 mins**
Short talk on the theme (*if appropriate*) or **Reading** – perhaps a poem or extract from a book could alternate with a reading from the Bible	**5 mins**
Silence, or quiet music, for reflection	**8 mins**
Intercessory prayer	**5 mins**
Hymn or Song	**3 mins**
Silence until the next half-hour begins	**5 mins**

PART II

Services you could use

1: CELEBRATION OF MARRIAGE

"COME TOGETHER"

The minister (ordained or lay) welcomes the people in these or other suitable words

> We have come together as the family of God
>   in our Father's presence
> to offer him praise and thanksgiving,
> to hear and receive his holy word,
> to bring before him the needs of the world,
> to ask his forgiveness of our sins,
> and to seek his grace,
> that through his Son, Jesus Christ
> we may give ourselves to his service.

HYMN or SONG OF PRAISE *(e.g. "Lord for the years", "Now thank we all our God", "Praise my soul, the King of heaven", or see suggestions in chapter 13)*

Remain standing for the
ACT OF PRAISE AND THANKSGIVING

Leader: God our Father, we praise you as we give you thanks
          for all your gifts to us and all your people:
          For beauty, truth and order in nature,
          in music and in the arts:
          God of grace

ALL: We give you thanks and praise.

Leader: For wholeness of life: in body, mind and spirit, and for the
          variety of our interests and abilities:
          God of grace

ALL: We give you thanks and praise

Leader: For freedom to think, to speak, to believe and worship as we will,
           freedom to travel and visit other places:
           God of grace
ALL: We give you thanks and praise

Leader: For our children, their joys and sorrows,
           and their ability to see what we cannot see:
           God of grace
ALL: We give you thanks and praise

Leader: For the communities in which we live and work;
           for health, shelter and safety,
           for food, warmth and security:
           God of grace
ALL: We give you thanks and praise

Leader: For our privileges and for the challenges they bring;
           for the work you have given us to do
           in our homes, our parishes and our communities:
           God of grace
ALL: We give you thanks and praise

Leader: For all who have shown us your love
           and helped us to faith in Christ crucified,
           for our parents, our teachers and for the Church:
           God of grace
ALL: We give you thanks and praise

Leader: And today, above all, we thank you for our love for each other,
           and the ways we express and receive that love:
           the pleasure of shared activities, and silent understanding,
           the satisfaction of giving, and the joy of physical union.
           We thank you for our homes and families:
           for the old and the young, those whom we need and those who
           need us: for all your generosity to us, God of grace
ALL: We give you thanks and praise

Remain standing to sing or say the Doxology
>Praise, God, from whom all blessings flow,
>Praise him, all creatures here below,
>Praise him above, ye heavenly host,
>Praise Father, Son and Holy Ghost.

THE WORD OF GOD

Sit for the first reading

(e.g. Genesis 1. 26-28 + 31a, Psalm 128, Matthew 7. 21 + 24-27,
Mark 10. 6-9, Luke 24. 13-35, John 2. 1-11, John 15. 9-12,
Romans 12. 1-2 +9-13, 1 Corinthians 13, Ephesians 3. 14,
Ephesians 5. 21-end, Colossians 3. 12-17, 1 John 4. 7-12)

All stand to sing a hymn or song relevant to the reading

*Sit for a second reading, either one of the above, or e.g. "Marriage" from
The Prophet (Kahlil Gibran), or for a dance or drama relating to marriage.*

THE ADDRESS

Sit or kneel for the

THE ACT OF INTERCESSION

Leader: God our Father, we pray for your people throughout the world:
          we pray for your Church,
          that we may share in the work of your Son,
          revealing you to women and men and children
          and reconciling them to you and to each other,
          so that all may love as you have loved us:
          Lord in your mercy

ALL: Receive our prayer

Leader: We pray for those who suffer
          for faith or conscience or truth,
          for those who are tempted to turn back:
          help them to know that they are not alone,

to hold out to the end,
and by their witness draw others to you:
Lord in your mercy

ALL: **Receive our prayer**

Leader: We pray for the nations of the world;
give peace where there is conflict, violence or oppression
peace between nations, among neighbours, and in our hearts:
Lord in your mercy

ALL: **Receive our prayer**

Leader: We pray for our own country,
and for all who carry responsibility in it:
that no-one may be exploited, neglected or forgotten,
and that all may work together for the common good:
Lord in your mercy

ALL: **Receive our prayer**

Leader: We pray for homes and families,
that husbands and wives may be faithful to their vows,
and children may be brought up to know and follow you;
give comfort to those who are divorced
and to all who live in broken or divided families;
we pray for those who live alone,
whether by choice or from necessity,
and for all who work to strengthen marriage and family life;
Lord in your mercy

ALL: **Receive our prayer**

Leader: We pray for those who are ill or disabled,
and all who are afraid or perplexed:
give them wholeness of body mind and spirit;
comfort those who are in any kind of trouble,
and sustain all who care for others:
Lord in your mercy

ALL: **Receive our prayer**

Leader: Finally we pray for our own homes and families,
           that they may be places of harmony, faith and growth;
           we pray for our parents, our brothers and sisters,
           our children, god-children and grandchildren,
           and especially those who live far away from us.
           We remember with gratitude those who have died;
           Merciful Father

ALL: **Accept these prayers for the sake of your Son,
           our Saviour Jesus Christ. Amen.**

THE ACT OF CONFESSION

**God of mercy,
we confess that we have turned away from you
and from each other;
we repent of our hasty actions,
our unkind words and bitter thoughts,
our greed our anger and our indifference;
we are sorry for our selfishness, and all our sins,
and ask for your forgiveness.**

Minister   Almighty God
           who forgives all who truly repent
           have mercy upon us,
           pardon and deliver us from all our sins,
           confirm and strengthen us in all goodness,
           and keep us in life eternal;
           through Jesus Christ our Lord. **Amen.**

Stand to sing A HYMN OR SONG ABOUT FAMILY LIFE (see chapter 13.3) during which the collection is taken, and then, if desired, symbols of family life can be presented with the following words

ALL: **God, our Father,**
these offerings are tokens of the whole of our lives;
with them we bring to you
our minds and bodies,
our talents and abilities,
our ambitions and plans for the future,
our work and our leisure,
our responsibilities and privileges,
our friendships and our family life,
our love for each other
and the joy and sadness that we share.
Give us grace to use all the gifts,
which you have so generously given to us,
that your glory may be proclaimed
and your will be done.

Minister: Almighty and most merciful Father,
who gave marriage to be a source of blessing,
we thank you for family life,
with all its joys and sorrows.
May we know your presence and peace in our homes;
fill them with your love and use them for your glory;
through Jesus Christ our Lord. **Amen.**

We gather up all our prayers in the prayer of the Family of God

The Lord's Prayer

Stand for THE BLESSING or **The Grace** *and THE FINAL HYMN.*

2: ANNIVERSARY OF MARRIAGE

with the option of renewal of vows and / or the giving and receiving of an eternity ring and / or a signet ring

WELCOME by the minister

A HYMN OR SONG may be sung

Minister: God is love, and those who live in love
            live in God; and God lives in them. *(1 John 4.16)*

            The Lord be with you
All: **And also with you**

Minister: God our Father you have taught us through your Son
            that love is the fulfilling of the law;
            grant to your servants .... and .... that, loving one another,
            they may continue in your love until their lives' end:
            through Jesus Christ our Lord. **Amen**

THE NATURE OF MARRIAGE
            We have come together in the presence of God
            to give thanks with ....and ....for ....years of married life,
            to ask his forgiveness for all that has been amiss,
            to share their joy, and ask God's blessing upon them.
            As our Lord, Jesus Christ, was himself a guest
            at the wedding in Cana of Galilee,
            so through his Spirit he is with us now.

            Marriage is a gift of God in creation
            and a means of his grace; it is given that a husband and wife
            may comfort and help each other, living faithfully together
            in times of need as well as in plenty,

in sadness and in joy, in sickness and in health;
it is given that with delight and tenderness
they may know each other in love;
[it is given that they may have children
and be blessed in caring for them, bringing them up
in accordance with God's will, to his praise and glory.]
In marriage a couple belong together
and live life in the community;
it is a way of life created and hallowed by God,
that all should honour.
Therefore we pray with them
that strengthened and guided by God
they may continue to fulfil his purpose for their life together.

Silence is kept for reflection on the years that have passed, and on shared experiences, good and bad.

The minister says to the couple
I invite you now to recall the vows that you made at your wedding

Husband: I .... took you .... to be my wife
Wife: I .... took you .... to be my husband
Together: to have and to hold from that day forward
for better, for worse, for richer, for poorer
in sickness and in health, to love and to cherish,
till death us do part, according to God's holy law
and this was our solemn vow.

Today, in the presence of our family and friends,
we affirm our continuing commitment to this vow.

If a ring (or rings) is to be given these words are used

.........., I give you this ring
as a sign of my life-long commitment to you
.........., I receive this ring
as a sign of my life-long commitment to you

[or, if not, both may touch the wedding ring(s) with the words
.........., I gave you this ring
as a sign of my life-long commitment to you
.........., I received this ring
as a sign of my life-long commitment to you]

Together: So may this ring (these rings) continue
to be a symbol of our giving and receiving,
together in endless love.

The couple kneel together while the minister says
God the Father, God the Son, God the Holy Spirit,
bless, preserve and keep you;
the Lord mercifully grant the riches of his grace
that you may please him both in body and soul,
and living together in faith and love,
may receive the blessings of eternal life. **Amen.**

Blessed are you, heavenly Father
All: **You give joy to husband and wife.**
Blessed are you, Lord Jesus Christ
All: **You have brought new life to mankind.**
Blessed are you, Holy Spirit of God
All: **You bring us together in love.**
Blessed be Father, Son and Holy Spirit
All: **One God, to be praised for ever. Amen**

*One or more readings from the Bible, or elsewhere may be used, a hymn
or psalm may be sung and / or a sermon preached*

Minister: Almighty God giver of life and love, bless .... and .... ;
grant them wisdom and devotion in their life together,
that each may continue to be to the other
a strength in need, a comfort in sorrow,
and a companion in joy.
So unite their wills in your will,
and their spirits in your Spirit,
that they may live in love and peace all the days of their life,
through Jesus Christ our Lord. **Amen.**

Almighty God, our heavenly Father,
who gave marriage to be a source of blessing,
we thank you for family life, with all its joys and sorrows.
May we know your presence and peace in our homes,
fill them with your love, and use them for your glory,
through Jesus Christ our Lord. **Amen.**

The Lord's Prayer

BLESSING

God the Holy Trinity make you strong in faith and love,
defend you on every side, and guide you in truth and peace;
and the blessing of God almighty,
the Father, the Son, and the Holy Spirit,
be among you and remain with you always. **Amen.**

*(The form of this service is based on one devised by Canon John Brown of Margaretting,
Essex, from The Marriage Service in the "Alternative Service Book " © 1980 The Central
Board of Finance of the Church of England and is reproduced with his permission)*

1: FAMILY LIFE - its ups and downs

Psalm 139 1-6 or 7-18

THANKSGIVING

Leader: Thank you, God, for this wonderful world,
             for all its sights and sounds
             that please us.

             Thank you for the sounds of human voices:
             whispering, speaking out loud,
             shouting, singing,
             giving expression to sorrow and joy,
             to prayer and praise;
             teaching, amusing,
             encouraging and guiding.

             Thank you for the sounds of human labour:
             turning wheels, banging hammers,
             roaring engines, ringing bells,
             whining sirens, clacking typewriters,
             and rattling pots and pans.

             Thank you for the sounds of nature:
             birds singing, sea-gulls calling,
             dogs barking, cats miaowing,
             cows mooing, horses neighing,
             the sea's roar, the rain's pour,
             the wind's whistle, the stream's ripple.

             Thank you, God, for these,
             and all the sounds that please us.
             Thank you, God, for the sounds of silence.

(Alan Gaunt from "New Prayers for Worship" ©John Paul, the Preachers Press)

LITANY OF INTERCESSIONS

Leader: We pray for the family of the Church, for loving relationships, and for the life of families around us, saying Jesus, Lord of love

ALL: **in your mercy, hear us.**

Leader: Jesus, you blessed marriage in the wedding at Cana of Galilee: be with those preparing for marriage, with all who lead marriage preparation, and with all who give marriage guidance. Jesus, Lord of love

ALL: **in your mercy, hear us.**

Leader: Jesus, you welcomed the little children who came to you: give understanding and patience to all who have the care of children. Jesus, Lord of love

ALL: **in your mercy, hear us.**

Leader: Jesus you did not condemn the woman taken in sin, but told her to "sin no more": forgive us our sins and strengthen us to lead new lives of love and service to our families and neighbours. Jesus, Lord of love

ALL: **in your mercy, hear us.**

Leader: Jesus, you healed Peter's mother-in-law: bring comfort and healing to all who are ill at home or in hospital, and to all their families; especially we ask you to heal broken relationships and divided families. Jesus, Lord of love

ALL: **in your mercy, hear us.**

Leader: Jesus you treated the rich young man with sympathy: help our young people as they work out their priorities for life: especially we pray for all young people in trouble, at home, in school or with the police. Jesus, Lord of love

ALL: **in your mercy, hear us.**

Leader: Jesus, on the cross you said "Mother, behold your son": comfort and strengthen all who are childless or bereaved, all orphans and widows, all who feel lonely or deserted. Jesus, Lord of love

ALL: **in your mercy, hear us.**

Leader: Jesus, you provided food for your disciples on the sea-shore: strengthen all who try to provide food, clothing and shelter for those who have none. Jesus, Lord of love

ALL: **in your mercy, hear us.**

Leader: Jesus, you were born in poverty and soon became a refugee: be with families today who have had to leave their homes to find food and safety. Jesus, Lord of love

ALL: **in your mercy, hear us.**

Leader: Jesus, you grew in wisdom and in favour with God and with people in the family of Mary and Joseph: bring wisdom and an awareness of the presence and love of God into our homes and families today. Jesus, Lord of love

ALL: **in your mercy, hear us.**

Leader: Jesus, you said that you are the bread of life, and left us the sacrament of your Body and Blood: bring your whole Church at last to the heavenly banquet with you. Jesus, Lord of love

ALL: **in your mercy, hear us.**

For suitable Bible Readings and Hymns or Songs see chapters 11 and 13. For further prayers for Family Life see the "Mothers' Union Prayer Book", and especially the Mothers' Union "Anthology of Public Prayers" pp.18, 23, 26, 32 and 38 - 49.

2: CHRISTIAN CONCERN FOR FAMILIES WORLDWIDE

based on the Five Objects of the Mothers' Union

WELCOME by the Leader

A HYMN can be sung

Leader: Rejoicing at the presence of God here among us,
let us pray in faith and trust

The Lord's Prayer

THE FIRST OBJECT

Leader: As members of the Mothers' Union, we have as our first Object
"to uphold Christ's teaching on the nature of Marriage and to
promote its wider understanding" So let us join together in a
prayer of thanksgiving for family life:

We thank God for giving us other people to be part of our lives
ALL: **We praise you, O Lord, and bring you thanks today**

For parents and the love which brought us to birth
ALL: **We praise you, O Lord, and bring you thanks today**

For mothers who have cherished and nurtured us
ALL: **We praise you, O Lord, and bring you thanks today**

For fathers who have loved and supported us
ALL: **We praise you, O Lord, and bring you thanks today**

For brothers and sisters with whom we have shared our home
ALL: **We praise you, O Lord, and bring you thanks today**

For children entrusted to our care
ALL: **We praise you, O Lord, and bring you thanks today**

For other relatives who have been with us
in our hopes and our struggles

ALL: **We praise you, O Lord, and bring you thanks today**

For all who have spoken to us of the love of Jesus
and have drawn us in to the family of the Church:

ALL: **Help us to live as people who belong to one another and to you.**

(from Church Family Worship © 1986 Jubilate Hymns Ltd)

Bible reading: e.g. Philippians 2. 1-11 or some other

THE SECOND OBJECT

Leader: As a reminder of our commitment to encourage parents to bring up their children in the life and the faith of the Church, we renew the promises made at our baptism, and which we have made for our children and godchildren:

Do you believe and trust in God the Father who made the world?

ALL: **I believe and trust in him.**

Do you believe and trust in his Son who redeemed the world?

ALL: **I believe and trust in him.**

Do you believe and trust in his Holy Spirit
who gives life to the people of God?

ALL: **I believe and trust in him.**

This is the faith of the Church.

ALL: **This is our faith: we believe and trust in one God, Father, Son and Holy Spirit.**

Leader: Almighty God,
whose Son equips the Church with a variety of gifts,

grant that we may use them to bear witness to Christ
by lives built on faith and love.
Make us ready to live his gospel
and eager to do his will
that we may share with all your Church
in the joys of eternal life;
through Jesus Christ our Lord. **Amen.**

THE THIRD OBJECT

Leader: The Mothers' Union is a worldwide fellowship united in prayer,
worship and service. We remind ourselves of the diversity of
God's creation, and the very different needs of everyone within
the world.
Let us pray that God will help us to be faithful in prayer, worship
and service:

Holy Spirit of unity and power,
we thank you for our fellowship with one another
as members of the Mothers' Union
in one Church across the world.
Teach us how to pray and serve you,
and how to encourage one another.
Lead us to see the opportunities
which you have prepared for us to serve each other. **Amen.**

The Mothers' Union Prayer

THE FOURTH AND FIFTH OBJECTS

Leader: The Mothers' Union is specifically concerned for stable family
            life and the protection of children. We celebrate family life, but
            we also need to confess to God those things in our lives that
            are against his will. As we confess our sins, we especially bring
            to God those people whose lives have met with adversity and
            been spoilt by the sin of others.

            For our unwillingness to give of ourselves,
            our bitterness, pride and desire for cheap revenge

ALL: **Forgive us, Lord.**

            For our failure to see our children as your children,
            and our desire to make them what we will, not what you will

ALL: **Forgive us, Lord.**

            For our concentration on our own family,
            so we forget the wider one,
            our lack of concern for other families,
            and our hasty judgements and intolerance of other ways of life

ALL: **Forgive us, Lord**

Leader: May God, our heavenly Father,
            who has promised to forgive all those who sincerely turn to him,
            have mercy on each one of us (you),
            deliver us from our sins,
            and strengthen us for his service;
            through Jesus Christ our Lord. **Amen.**

ACT OF DEDICATION

Reader: The sovereign Lord has filled me with his Spirit.
He has chosen me and sent me
to bring good news to the poor,
to heal the broken-hearted,
to announce release to captives
and recovery of sight to the blind.
He has sent me to proclaim
that the time has come
when the Lord will save his people
and defeat their enemies.
He has sent me to comfort all who mourn,
to give to those who mourn in Zion
joy and gladness instead of grief,
a song of praise instead of sorrow.
They will be like trees
which the Lord himself has planted.
They will all do what is right,
and God will be praised for what he has done.
(Isaiah 61. 1-3)

ALL: Father,
we dedicate ourselves to serve you faithfully
and to follow Christ,
to face the future with him,
seeking his special purpose for our lives.
Send us out now to work and witness freely,
gratefully and full of hope,
in the power of the Holy Spirit
and to the honour and glory of your name. Amen.

PRAYERS can be said here for families in adversity, or for particular problems in local, or national life, or in different parts of the world.

A HYMN can be sung

Leader: Lord, you experienced the pattern of family life;
           we ask that our families may learn
           to live together in love, respect and forgiveness.
           In times of difficulty, strengthen us;
           in times of perplexity, bring us wisdom;
           in times of happiness, make us thankful.

           And may the blessing of God,
           the Father, the Son and the Holy Spirit
           be with us and with those we love, now and always. **Amen.**

3: MOTHERING SUNDAY SERVICES

INTRODUCTION

Mothering Sunday is included in this service book because clergy often turn to the Mothers' Union leaders and branches to make the arrangements for such worship.

Mothering Sunday services are of two kinds:

❋   the usual Sunday service, probably in the morning, with or without Holy Communion, but with specially chosen readings, prayers and music, or

❋   a service at a different time, probably in the afternoon, using a form specially put together for the occasion.

In many churches it is customary to give out posies, or small bunches of flowers to the children to give to their mothers, or for everybody there to take one to whoever may be at home, or to give flowers to all the women in the congregation. Alternatively the children may make flower cards or greeting cards if they have separate activity time, or bake a Simnel or other cake, for distribution at the end of the service.

One of the difficulties about Mothering Sunday is the number and variety of ideas which are inherent: the history of the "Mothers' Day" concept stresses the idea of the children away "in service" having a spring "holy-day" off and walking home (perhaps several miles) from the big house, picking flowers for their mother from the hedgerows as they go. The Book of Common Prayer epistle for Lent 4 contains the idea of the Holy City, Jerusalem "the mother of us all" and so the Church as "Mother Church". Years ago this was often recognised by people going to worship at the Mother Church of the diocese, the cathedral.

The two-year lectionary used extensively throughout the Anglican Communion has "The Transfiguration" as its theme for the day. *The Common Lectionary* (three-year, ecumenical) makes no reference to Mothering Sunday. The Lenten mood of suffering and penitence is sometimes maintained by concentrating on the suffering of Mary as the season draws us nearer to the passion of Our Lord; this is often chosen as the focus when Lent 4 falls close to March 25th and the celebration of the Annunciation. Other themes can be "Mary as the model mother", "Honour your parents", "Family relationships". It is necessary for anyone arranging a special service for "Mothering Sunday" to be selective about which one of these ideas they want to use, and not try and include too much.

In many ways the principles which apply in the preparation and conduct of Pram Services are relevant when arranging a service for Mothering Sunday, although the children present will probably be older, and there may be more fathers and grandparents present. Bearing in mind that many people will come on Mothering Sunday who are not regular church attenders, of particular importance will be

☀️   the welcome given at the beginning of the service

☀️   a brief explanation at the beginning of what will happen, and what the service is trying to do

☀️   thorough preparation of all the material, and of all the people who will take part in the service

☀️   the level of activity needed in the service to involve chidren and hold everyone's interest.

There are a number of publications which can help with the content of Mothering Sunday services within the framework of a standard Service of the Word, especially the themes in the Church House Publishing booklets

Our Mum (1975) and *Flowers, Fonts and Fuzzies* (1986), section 14 in *Church Family Worship*, and the relevant sections in *For All the Family* and *More for All the Family* etc. (see *Books and Addresses* in the chapter of Resources). For a eucharistic service there is alternative material in *Enriching the Christian Year.*

An example is given here of a service which can be used in a special service e.g. on Mothering Sunday afternoon or as a Family Service in the morning. It is followed by a form of intercession taken from *Enriching the Christian Year* and other prayers especially suitable for Mothering Sunday.

A: *SIMPLE SERVICE*

Before the service begins the flowers, cards, packets of seeds, biscuits, cakes, or whatever is to be given out, should be placed ready to be carried up to the front by the children.

The person leading the service welcomes everyone, and explains what is going to happen during the service and tells people if refreshments are being served afterwards. It is probably best if everyone stays sitting down except when they stand to sing.

Leader:	Let us praise the Lord
ALL:	**The Lord be praised**
Leader:	He gives us life
ALL:	**The Lord be praised**
Leader:	He loves and helps us
ALL:	**The Lord be praised**

All sing the first hymn or song

Leader: Our heavenly Father in his love gave Jesus to the world.
           He grew up in the family of Mary and Joseph.
           Each week on their holy day, when they sat down for supper

Mary would light the candles, and say a prayer for the family. We are here together as the family of God, so we ask one of the mothers to light the candles for us today.

The candles are lit

Leader: Jesus is the light of the world;
            he shines in the dark, and shows us the way to live.
            Glory be to you, Father, Son and Holy Spirit.
            You have made us to live in loving families.
            Be with us in our homes, and bless us here today.

ALL: **Amen.**

Leader: Let us listen now to the story about a boy who gave his food
            to Jesus who shared it with five thousand hungry people.

Reader: John 6. 3-11

            The word of the Lord

ALL: **Thanks be to God**

The leader invites the children to bring the gifts to the front, where they should be displayed on a table, where everyone can see them.

THANKSGIVING

Leader: God our Father,
            we thank you for all that you have given us:
            for the food we eat, and those who prepare it for us

ALL: **Thank you, Father**

Leader: for giving us gifts we can share with other people

ALL: **Thank you, Father**

Leader: for all who love and care for us, and for our homes

ALL: **Thank you, Father**

Leader: for our families and friends and teachers

ALL: **Thank you, Father**
Leader: for our faith in Jesus Christ,
                  and our hope of living in your love
ALL: **Thank you, Father**

Stand to sing a hymn or song

Leader: Let us listen to what Jesus said about children

Reader: Luke 18. 15-17

                  The word of the Lord
ALL: **Thanks be to God**

A short talk, or act, or a song, could be included here.

PRAYERS OF INTERCESSION

*These or other simple prayers are said by the leader, or by older children,
or by a family together*

For mothers
                  Lord Jesus,
                  as your mother Mary cared for you
                  throughout your earthly life,
                  so may all mothers care for their children,
                  giving comfort and courage, praise and advice,
                  sharing laughter and tears.
                  Help them to be patient and understanding:
                  to know when to act and when to stand back,
                  so that their children may grow up
                  to know your love and presence in their lives.
                  Lord Jesus, hear our prayer.

For family life

Father in heaven,
we pray for the homes and family life
of all who are here today:
help us to care for each other
and to take the trouble both
to talk and to listen to each other.
Help us not only to forgive and forget
but also to be willing to apologise
and to receive forgiveness.
We pray in the name of Jesus Christ, our Redeemer.

For those whose family life is difficult

Father we pray for all unhappy families;
give healing where children or parents are ill or in hospital;
strengthen mothers and fathers
who cannot provide for their children;
give comfort where parents are separated
or children have run away or are in trouble;
be with all who are alone or lonely;
we ask in the name of Jesus.

For the Church

Almighty God,
we pray for the family of the Church;
that all Christians may work together in harmony
for the spread of the Gospel of Jesus Christ,
and the building up of your people.

For the world

O God, the Father of us all,
direct the leaders of the world that all your children
may live together in justice and in peace.
We pray that fighting and war may come to an end.
We pray particularly for ....

Leader: As our Saviour Jesus Christ has taught us
           so we say together the Family prayer

ALL: **The Lord's Prayer**

*The leader explains that in the next hymn the children come forward to
receive the gifts and give them to their mothers / parents or take them
home to them. Any gifts that are left may be taken by older people to give
to their mothers, wives or sisters, or to people who are ill.*

All stand to sing a hymn or song

Leader: Father in heaven,
           as we put out the candles at the end of our service,
           we remember that we are each called
           to shine as a light to the world.
           So we give ourselves to you:
           set us on fire with your love,
           to shine for you and do your will,
           through Jesus Christ your son.

ALL: **May the grace of our Lord Jesus Christ,
           the love of God, and the fellowship of the Holy Spirit,
           be with us and remain with us always. Amen.**

B: *PRAYERS FOR MOTHERING SUNDAY*
(*for use with or without Communion*)

Collect

God of compassion,
whose Son, Jesus Christ, the child of Mary,
shared the life of a home in Nazareth,
and on the cross drew the whole human family to himself:
strengthen us in our daily living
that in our joys and sorrows
we may know your presence to bind us together and to heal;
through Jesus Christ our Lord,
who is alive and reigns with you and the Holy Spirit,
one God, now and for ever. **Amen.**

Intercession

Leader: We pray for the family of the Church
and for the life of families around us, saying
Father of all

ALL: hear your children's prayer

Leader: Sovereign Lord, your Son has revealed you as our heavenly
Father, from whom every family in heaven and on earth is
named. Father of all

ALL: hear your children's prayer

Leader: You have made your Church a spiritual family, a household of
faith. Through baptism we are reborn as the brothers and
sisters of Christ; deepen our unity and fellowship in him.
Father of all

ALL: hear your children's prayer

Leader: You sent your Son to give his life a ransom for the whole human family. Give justice, peace and racial harmony to the world he died to save. Father of all

ALL: **hear your children's prayer**

Leader: You gave your Son a share in the life of a family in Nazareth. Help us to value our families, to be thankful for them, and to live sensitively within them. Father of all

ALL: **hear your children's prayer**

Leader: Your Son drew round him a company of friends. Bring love and joy to all who are alone. Help us all to find in the brothers and sisters of Christ a loving family. Father of all

ALL: **hear your children's prayer**

Leader: You are the God of the dead as well as of the living. In confidence we remember those of the household of faith who have gone before us. Bring us with them to the joy of your home in heaven, where you are alive and reign now and for ever. **Amen.**

(from Enriching the Christian Year © 1993 SPCK/ Triangle)

MORNING

A: GOD'S FAMILY - The whole company of heaven

PREPARATION

Leader: God has promised us that when two or three are gathered
            together in his name, he will be there among them, so we pray

                    Holy God,
                    help us to draw near to you in this time of prayer,
                    that we may worship you with all our hearts,
                    with all our minds, and with all our strength,
                    and that we may love and serve our neighbours
                    in everything we do. **Amen**

THE WORD OF GOD

Bible Reading: St Luke 11. 1-13, Ephesians 3. 14-20,
                    Revelation 7. 2-4+9 *or other appropriate reading.*

INTERCESSION

Leader: United in the company of all the faithful,
            and looking for the coming of the kingdom,
            let us offer our prayers to God,
            the source of all life and holiness.

            Merciful Lord,
            strengthen all Christian people by your Holy Spirit,
            that we may live as a royal priesthood and a holy nation,
            to the praise of Christ Jesus our Saviour.
            Lord, hear our prayer
ALL: **In your mercy hear us**

Leader: Bless our bishops, and all ministers of your Church.....
that by faithful proclamation of your word we may be built,
on the foundation of the apostles and prophets,
into a holy temple of the Lord.
Lord, hear our prayer

ALL: **In your mercy hear us**

Leader: Give us power by the gift of your Holy and life-giving Spirit
that we may be transformed
into the likeness of Christ from glory to glory.
Lord, hear our prayer

ALL: **In your mercy hear us**

Leader: Hasten the day when those who fear you in every nation
will come from east and west, from north and south,
and sit at table in your kingdom.
Lord, hear our prayer

ALL: **In your mercy hear us**

Leader: Give to the world and its peoples
the peace that comes from above,
that they may find Christ's way of freedom and life.
Lord, hear our prayer

ALL: **In your mercy hear us**

Leader: Touch and heal all those whose lives are scarred by sin,
or disfigured by pain,
that, raised from death to life in Christ,
their sorrow may be turned to eternal joy.
Lord, hear our prayer

ALL: **In your mercy hear us**

Leader: Remember in your mercy those gone before us
who have been well-pleasing to you from eternity;
preserve us who live here by faith,
guide us to your kingdom,

and grant us your peace at all times.
Lord, hear our prayer

ALL: **In your mercy hear us**

Leader: And so we give you thanks
for the whole company of your saints in glory,
with whom in fellowship we join our prayers and praises;
by your grace may we, like them,
be made perfect in your love.
Lord, hear our prayer

ALL: **In your mercy hear us**

(from General Synod Prayers for 1994 ©Central Board of Finance of the Church of England)

Leader: O Lord our God, listening to us here,
you accept also the prayers of our sisters and brothers
in Africa, Asia, the Pacific, the Americas and Europe,
we are all one in prayer.
So may we, as one, rightly carry out your commission
to witness and to love in the Church
and throughout the world.
Accept our prayers graciously,
even when they are somewhat strange;
they are offered in Jesus' name. **Amen.**

(from Ghana, included in "A Wee Worship Book" ©1989 The Iona Community)

Leader: Let us pray for the unity of all peoples on earth
in the words our Saviour has taught us

The Lord's Prayer

The Mothers' Union Prayer

Leader: O God, who has called us in Christ to be members of your family, the Church: give us such love towards each other that the world may see in our common life a reflection of your love for us all; through Jesus Christ our Lord. **Amen.**

(from FLAME International Year of the Family material)

The Grace

B: "UNITED IN PRAYER AND WORSHIP" - from Kenya

PREPARATION

Leader: We have come together, the people of God,
            drawn by his Spirit, longing for his word,
            to praise the holy name of the Lord,
            to share the glorious news of grace,
            to pray for our needs and the pains of the world,
            to rejoice in his love and be sent in his peace.

Leader: We are heirs of the Father
ALL: **joint heirs with the Son**
Leader: renewed in the Spirit
ALL: **together we are one.**

THE WORD OF GOD

An appropriate verse of Scripture may be said

Leader: Lord have mercy
ALL: **Lord have mercy**
Leader: Christ have mercy
ALL: **Christ have mercy**
Leader: Lord have mercy
ALL: **Lord have mercy**

Leader: Blessed are those who live in your house
ALL: **they will be always singing your praise.**
Leader: Praise the Lord
ALL: **The name of the Lord be praised**

Either
Leader: The glorious Son of God on high
ALL: **is born for us through Mary's womb:**

Leader:	The homeless Prince of Peace on earth
ALL:	**is crushed and lies in Joseph's tomb**
Leader:	The reigning Lord of life and death
ALL:	**breaks the bond of time and doom.**

Or the following

Leader:	Glory to the Father in whom all things began,
ALL:	**Glory to the Son who became the Son of Man,**
	Glory to the Spirit who inspires and renews.
	The Lord our God for ever! Alleluia!

JUBILATE SONG

I will enter his gates with thanksgiving in my heart;
I will enter his courts with praise.
I will say this is the day that the Lord has made;
I will rejoice for he has made me glad.
He has made me glad, he has made me glad;
I will rejoice for he has made me glad.
He has made me glad, he has made me glad;
I will rejoice for he has made me glad.

THE SONG OF THE MESSIAH
(Genesis 12. 3, Deuteronomy 18. 15f, 2 Samuel 7. 12f, Isiaiah 53. 4)

Jesus, the seed of Abraham, blesses the nations;
Jesus, the prophet, like Moses, frees the oppressed:
Jesus, the Lord of King David, leads the people:
Jesus, the Servant of the Lord, suffers and saves:
Jesus, the Son of Man, was crucified and raised.
Glory...

or

THE SONG OF JESUS

(Luke 6. 27, Matthew 25. 35-6, Luke 7. 22-23, Luke 10. 21)

ALL: **Love your enemies,**
do good to those who hate you,

Leader: bless those who curse you,
pray for those who abuse you.

I was hungry and you gave me food,
thirsty and you gave me drink,

a stranger and you welcomed me,
naked and you clothed me,

sick and you visited me
in prison and you came to me.

The blind receive their sight,
the lame walk, the lepers are cleansed.

The deaf hear, the dead are raised:
the good news is preached to the poor
and blessed are those not offended at me.

ALL: **Love your enemies,**
do good to those who hate you,

Glory...

PRAYERS

Leader: United in prayer with our brothers and sisters throughout the
world, we say together

The Lord's Prayer

Leader:	Show us your mercy, O Lord
ALL:	**and grant us your salvation.**
Leader:	O Lord, guide our Queen / president / prime minister
ALL:	**and give our leaders wisdom and justice.**
Leader:	May your ministers serve you faithfully
ALL:	**and your royal people joyfully**
Leader:	In the valley of the shadow of death;
ALL:	**protect us with your rod and staff.**
Leader:	Like trees planted by the waterside;
ALL:	**grant us the fruit of your Spirit.**
Leader:	Send us out as the salt of the earth;
ALL:	**and as the light of the world.**
Leader:	May the earth be filled with your glory;
ALL:	**as the waters cover the sea.**

Leader: Almighty and everlasting God,
Father of the Prince of Peace,
in returning and rest we are saved,
in quietness and trust is our strength.
Grant us the blessing of making peace,
and the joy of seeking justice.
Take from our souls the strain and stress,
and let our ordered lives confess,
the beauty of your peace;
through Jesus Christ our Lord. **Amen.**

Prayerful choruses or a hymn may be sung. People may join in open prayers for contemporary, personal, national or world needs, or use some of the following:

The Mothers' Union Prayer

For the Church

Almighty and eternal God,
the only source of power;
grant to our bishops, our clergy
and all the people of our churches
your health-giving Spirit of grace;
and, that we may truly please you,
pour on us the continual dew of your blessing.
Grant this for the sake of our advocate
and mediator, Jesus Christ. **Amen.**

For mission and evangelism

O God our Father,
give us a passion for your Word
and boldness in telling our neighbour
about your grace.
May the Holy Spirit convict the lost
and draw them to the Saviour,
Jesus Christ our Lord. **Amen.**

For life in towns and cities

Creator God, our heavenly Father,
your Son was a carpenter in Nazareth,
with nowhere to lay his head;
we pray for all those who labour
in our factories and shops.
Grant them wisdom and honesty, strength and skill,
to provide for themselves
and for the needs of our country.
Look with compassion on the poor,
the unemployed and homeless,
the orphans and the hungry,
and grant us your power to work towards justice
in transforming their lives for your glory;
through our risen Lord Jesus Christ. **Amen.**

For guidance

> Guide us, Lord, in all we do
> with your grace and love,
> and grant us your continual help;
> that in all our works,
> begun, continued and ended in you,
> we may glorify your holy name,
> and by your mercy attain everlasting life,
> through Jesus Christ our Lord. **Amen.**

The Grace...

(This order of service is adapted from "A Service of Morning Prayer" in "Modern Services" ©1991 the Church of the Province of Kenya)

C: "YOU SHALL BE MY WITNESSES"

PREPARATION

Sentence:
Jesus said: "All authority in heaven and on earth has been given to me. Go,
therefore, and make disciples of all peoples". *(Matthew 29. 18-19) or*
Jesus said: "you shall receive power when the Holy Spirit has come upon
you, and you shall be my witnesses". *(Acts 1.8)*

INVITATION TO PRAISE (from Psalm 98)

Leader:	Sing to the Lord, all the world,
ALL:	**for the Lord is a mighty God.**
Leader:	Sing a new song to the Lord,
ALL:	**for he has done marvellous things.**
Leader:	Proclaim his glory among the nations,
ALL:	**and shout for joy to the Lord our King!**
	Glory to the Father and to the Son,
	and to the Holy Spirit,
	As it was in the beginning is now,
	and shall be for ever, Amen.

A Hymn or Song of Praise may be sung

PENITENCE
*(people should be asked to respond to the prompt "be merciful" with the
words **"Lord, forgive us and help us"**)*

Leader:	Lord God, our maker and redeemer, this is your world and we are your people: come among us and save us. Where we have heard for ourselves the good news of Christ, but have not shared it with our generation nor taught it to our children, be merciful:
ALL:	**Lord, forgive us and help us.**

Leader: Where we have failed to bring the love of Christ to the needy in our society, be merciful:

ALL: Lord, forgive us and help us.

Leader: Where we have not loved you with all our heart, nor our neighbours as ourselves, be merciful:

ALL: Lord, forgive us and help us.

Leader: O God, forgive us our lack of love, and in your mercy make us what you would have us to be, through Jesus Christ our Lord. **Amen.**

Almighty God,
who on the day of Pentecost,
sent your Holy Spirit to the disciples
with the wind from heaven and tongues of flame,
filling them with joy and boldness to preach the Gospel:
send us out in the power of the same Spirit
to witness to your truth
and to draw all people to the fire of your love;
through Jesus Christ our Lord. **Amen.**

(Collect for Pentecost from the "Alternative Service Book " © 1980 The Central Board of Finance of the Church of England)

READING(S)
e.g. Jeremiah 1. 1-8, Matthew 28. 10-20, Mark 1. 16-20 + 3. 13-19, John 15. 16-17, Acts 1. 6-8, Acts 5. 29-33.

A Song or Hymn can be sung

CREED

Leader: Let us proclaim the mystery of our faith:

ALL: **We believe in one Lord Jesus Christ -**
revealed in the flesh,
attested by the Spirit,
seen by apostles,
proclaimed to the nations,
believed in throughout the world,
and taken up to glory. Amen
(from 1 Timothy 3)

PRAYERS
(these or other prayers may be said by the leader or by other people)

God of all who journey,
we thank you for bringing us safely to this place.
We thank you for this opportunity of worshipping together.
You have brought us here
from different geographical points,
different theological points
and from different points of experience.
We pray that your Spirit will guide us (this morning /
today / throughout our conference)
to journey together across the boundaries that divide us:
the boundaries that we fear,
the boundaries that enthuse and excite us
but which demand that we take risks.
Bless us as we are gathered here with you
and allow us to proclaim your kingdom;
we ask in Jesus's name. **Amen.**
(Revd Janice Jones, Bangor)

O Lord God we are called to be your witnesses:
help us to make our saviour Jesus known to others -
through our words and lives,
through our prayers and the use of our gifts;
for his sake. **Amen.**

God most holy,
we give you thanks for bringing us
out of the shadow of night to the light of morning;
we ask you for the joy of spending this day in your service,
so that when evening comes,
we may once more give you thanks,
through Jesus Christ, your Son, our Lord. **Amen**.

(Reprinted by permission of the General Synod Office of the Scottish Episcopal Church)

Lord God, we thank you for our heritage of faith:
for the vision of the evangelists and apostles,
the courage of martyrs,
the conviction of teachers and preachers,
the devotion of family and friends,
and for all who have shown us your love,
and nourished us in the faith.
We thank you for the freedom
to talk about what we believe,
and to share it with our neighbours;
give us the will to recognise opportunities
to speak naturally about you,
and the courage and strength
to help others find faith.
through Jesus Christ our Lord. **Amen.**

God our Father, we dedicate ourselves
to serve you faithfully and to follow Christ:
send us out to work and witness freely,
gratefully and hopefully,
in the power of the Holy Spirit,
and for the honour and glory of your Son,
Jesus Christ our Lord. **Amen.**

The Grace

MID-DAY

A: FOR FAMILY LIFE

PREPARATION

O God, make speed to save us.
O Lord, make haste to help us.

Glory....

A HYMN, SONG OR PSALM may be sung

THE WORD OF GOD

PSALMODY
Parts of Psalm 119 (especially verses 1-8, 9-16, 33-40, 89-96, 97-104 or 145-152) or Psalms 127 or 128 *may be read, or said together.*

READING
One of the following, or some other
Genesis 1. 27-28a or Song of Songs 7. 10-13 - marriage
Ruth 1. 16-18 or 1 Samuel 18. 1-5 - alternative life commitments
Luke 2. 36-38 or Matthew 19. 10-12 - being single
Mark 10. 13-16 or 1 Samuel 2. 18-21 - infancy, childhood, youth
Luke 2. 41-45 or 2 Timothy 1. 2-5 - parenthood
Ecclesiastes 12. 1-8 or Genesis 49. 29-33 - old age, bereavement
Genesis 21. 9-14 or Genesis 44. 25-31 - broken families

or the short reading
Whoever does the will of God is my brother and sister and mother.
(Mark 3.35)

THE RESPONSE

Either

Leader: I bow my knees before the Father

ALL: From whom every family takes its name.

Leader: May we be strengthened in our inner being

ALL: With power through the Holy Spirit.

Leader: May Christ dwell in our hearts by faith

ALL: As we are being rooted and grounded in love

Leader: May we know the love of Christ that surpasses
            knowledge

ALL: And be filled with all the fullness of God.

or

Leader: That which we heard from the beginning

**ALL: Which we saw with our own eyes
            and touched with our hands,**

Leader: The Word of life, which was from the beginning,

ALL: We now proclaim to you.

Leader: The darkness is passing away

ALL: And the true light is already shining

Leader: God is our light, in whom there is no darkness at all.

ALL: If we walk in the light, we have fellowship with Christ.

PRAYERS

*Either a prayer on the topic of the reading, the KYRIES, or one of these
collects*:

> Loving God,
> from birth to death, you hold us in your hand:
> make us strong to bear each others burdens
> and humble to share our own,
> that as one family
> we may rest in your power
> and trust in your love;
> through Jesus Christ our Lord. **Amen.**

Almighty God
you have shed upon us
the new light of your incarnate word,
give us gladness in our sorrow
and a presence in our isolation:
fill our lives with your light
until they overflow with gladness and with praise;
through Jesus Christ our Saviour. **Amen.**

or **the Mothers' Union Prayer**

The Lord's Prayer
may be used, with this or some other introduction (chapter 13.1)

Leader: Rejoicing in the presence of God here among us,
           let us pray in faith and trust
           Our Father in heaven

Leader: May Christ dwell in our hearts by faith. **Amen**

Leader: Let us bless the Lord.
ALL: **Thanks be to God.**

(This service is based on Midday Prayer for Wednesday from "Celebrating Common Prayer"
©1992 The European Province of the Society of Saint Francis)

B: WITH THE WAVE OF PRAYER

At mid-day we remember Christ on the cross, and recall the glory of the ascended Christ at the time when the sun is at its height; coming as it does in the middle of the day's work, we are reminded to offer the whole of our life to God. It is a help to tell people in advance about life in the dioceses mentioned, and the work there of the Mothers' Union.

Leader: O God make speed to save us.
**ALL: O Lord make haste to help us.
            Glory to the Father...**

One or more of the following psalm(s) can be said together or by a reader
Psalm 19. 1-6, a section of Psalm 119, Psalm 121, 122, 126 or 130.
At the end of the psalm silence may be kept, or a prayer be said.

Leader: O God, the source of all life,
            you fill the earth with beauty:
            open our eyes to see your gracious hand in all your works,
            that rejoicing in your whole creation,
            we may learn to serve you with gladness,
            for the sake of him through whom all things were made,
            your Son, our Saviour and Lord, Jesus Christ. **Amen.**

A short passage of Scripture can be read:
e.g. Luke 1. 37-38, John 15. 12-17, Romans 5. 5,
2 Corinthians 5. 17-18, or 1. John 4. 7.

Reader: This is the word of the Lord.
ALL: Thanks be to God

Silence may be kept, and then two or more of the following prayers be used:

Leader: O God our Creator,
             we ask you to bless the work
             of the Mothers' Union throughout the world,
             and especially in each of the dioceses
             for which we pray today.........

             Bless our members in their lives and in their homes,
             that they, being strengthened in love to you,
             and to each other,
             may serve you faithfully to your glory,
             through Jesus Christ our Lord. **Amen.**

             Blessed Saviour,
             at this hour, you hung upon the cross,
             stretching out your loving arms:
             grant that we may look to you and be saved;
             for your tender mercies' sake. **Amen.**

             O Saviour of the world,
             who by your cross and precious blood have redeemed us;
             save us and help us, we humbly pray.

             Bless us now, Lord, in the middle of the day:
             be with us and with all who are dear to us,
             and with everyone we meet.
             Keep us true to you and joyful,
             simple and loving in all we do. **Amen.**

C: A SHORT FORM *for use during committee meetings*

For the Worldwide Mothers' Union

O God our heavenly Father,
we ask you to bless the work
of the Mothers' Union throughout the world,
and especially in each diocese for which we pray today........
Bless our members in their lives and in their homes,
that they, being strengthened in love to you,
and to each other,
may serve you faithfully, to your glory,
through Jesus Christ our Lord, **Amen.**

For today's meeting

Jesus, our Saviour:
you knew the pain of hard work and long hours
both in Nazareth and in your ministry with your disciples;
renew us now in our meeting here:
help us to hear other people's points of view,
and to discern your will as we make decisions;
grant us vision, discernment, courage and generosity.
When our meeting is over,
give patience and loyalty to all who disagree,
discretion about what has been discussed,
and diligence to those who have to carry out
what has been decided. **Amen.**

Lord of all eagerness, Lord of all faith,
Whose strong arms were skilled at the plane and the lathe:
Be here at our labours and give us, we pray
Your strength in our hearts, Lord, at the noon of the day.
(Jan Struther 1901-53)

For the coming of the kingdom of God

> Holy Spirit of God,
> fill us with your power,
> that in all we do and say,
> we may show forth the love of God the Father,
> and proclaim the good news of the kingdom
> to the peoples of the world;
> we ask in the name of Jesus Christ,
> our Lord and Saviour. **Amen.**

AFTERNOON OR EVENING

A: EVENING PRAYER *Suitable for use before an evening meeting, or a conference*

Leader: We have come together to enjoy each others' company
and to *(learn about … / hear about … / discuss … / plan …)*
For many of us the day has been busy:
for some a day packed with happiness and enjoyment;
for others perhaps a day of strain or sadness.
We know we are in the presence of God,
so we are quiet to honour him,
and reflect in silence on what the day has held ......

Two or three of the following prayers may be used, or some others, e.g. from the Mothers' Union "Anthology of Public Prayers", or from elsewhere in this book.

For our families

Heavenly Father,
we thank you for our families:
our parents and brothers and sisters,
our wives and husbands and our children,
our other relations, and family friends,
and all whom we love.
We bring before you now those members of our families
who need your help or comfort:
those who are ill or in hospital ....
those who are in trouble ....
all who have difficult decisions to make;
help us to see what we can do for them
and give us the strength and courage to do it;
through Jesus Christ our Lord. **Amen.**

For words - spoken and written

God our Father,
we praise and thank you for the gift of words:
the words we hear and read,
the words we speak and write.
As we communicate with others
help us to be sensitive to their circumstances
and responsible in our use of words,
that nothing we say or do
may cause hurt or harm to other people.
We thank you for the gift of your holy Word:
help us to read or listen to it every day,
so that we may learn and understand more and more
of your great love for us,
and may be able to see both your will for us
and the way to fulfil it.
We ask in the name of Jesus our Saviour. **Amen.**

For our meeting

Father,
as we meet together, help us to listen,
to understand and to remember.
Make us aware that we are meeting
not simply with each other, but with you:
make your presence real to each one of us.
As we listen help us to concentrate
so we hear what is intended
and what is your will.
Give us courage to say what needs to be said
and humility to accept decisions
with which we do not agree;
when we finish our meeting,
enable us by your grace,

to go out and fulfil your purpose,
doing what you want us to do;
and to your name be the glory,
through Jesus Christ our Lord. **Amen.**

For a new leader, minister or incumbent

Almighty God, our heavenly Father,
whose Son, Jesus Christ, humbled himself
to be the servant of all;
give us grace that as ....
comes to lead us (in our parish)
we may be guided by your Holy Spirit
to work together in peace and harmony,
so that this place
may be a beam of light to your glory
and to the furtherance of your kingdom;
through the example of our Lord and Saviour Jesus Christ,
who is our strength and hope
now and for the days to come.

(The Mothers' Union, Province of Ireland from "Women at Prayer')

For God's presence

Lord, when you seem far away, draw near to us;
when we are afraid, lighten our darkness;
when we are down, lift us up;
this we ask in your dear name.

(Guildford Diocese, England from "Women at Prayer")

For this house

The Father is in the house
Nothing need we fear

Christ is in the house
Loving us so dear

The Spirit is in the house
Listening to our prayer

The Three are in the house
Always very near.

(David Adam from "The Edge of Glory" ©Triangle / SPCK)

For civil leaders

Almighty God who created this world
and entrusted it to the children of men,
we ask you to give its rulers
the wisdom from above and goodwill to lead it
with justice, righteousness and truth.
Deliver us, we pray, from faithlessness and fear;
save us from fighting and wars
which are more and more driving our nations
to darkness, despair and misery.
Raise up Christian rulers, we pray O Lord,
and strengthen those rulers
who strive after unity and brotherhood,
and risk their lives to establish righteousness and peace
in the time when most people are striving after their own glory,
using the weapons of division.
Dear Lord, break down all barriers
which divide the rulers from the ruled,
that they may walk and work together
with each other and with you.
We pray trusting in you, Lord.

(Byumba Diocese, Rwanda from "Women at Prayer")

For peace

Heavenly Father,
maker of all things and giver of life,
have mercy on all the nations of the world.
Send down your abundant peace on every creature.
Let there be calm where there is violence;
peace where there is war;
freedom where there is bondage;
love and unity where there is strife;
abundance of food where there is starvation;
good health where there is sickness;
and life where there is death.
These and other good things we ask of you
through Jesus Christ our Lord.

(Mrs J.A. Ibimodi, Kwara Diocese, Nigeria from "Women at Prayer")

B: A SERVICE OF LIGHT

"The Service of Light was primarily a thanksgiving for the light, and a celebration of Christ our light, performed at home as well as in church." (Introduction in "The Promise of His Glory").

While usually considered to be a way to precede or start Evening Prayer, it may be used as a complete short service of prayer and praise, with readings and / or music or silence.

The Leader says one or more of the following, and the people respond

Leader: You, O Lord, are my lamp
ALL: You turn our darkness into light.
Leader: With you, O Lord, is the well of life:
ALL: In your light shall we see light.
Leader: Your word is a lantern to my feet
ALL: and a light upon our path.

Leader: In the beginning was the Word
           and the Word was with God, and the Word was God.
           He was in the beginning with God;
           all things were made through him,
           and without him was not anything made that was made.
           In him was life, and the life was the light of men.
           The light shines in the darkness,
           and the darkness has not overcome it. *(John 1. 1-5)*

A candle can be lit, with the words

Leader: Jesus Christ is the Light of the world
ALL: a light no darkness can quench.

*A hymn, psalm or song can be sung or said together or in parts
(see suggestions at the end)*

Leader: Let us give thanks to the Lord our God,
ALL: **He is worthy of all thanksgiving and praise.**

Leader: Blessed are you, Lord our God, King of the universe!
           Your word brings dawn in the morning,
           and brings on the dusk at evening,
           your wisdom creates both night and day.
           You determine the cycles of time,
           arrange the succession of seasons,
           and establish the stars in their heavenly courses.
           Lord of the starry hosts is your name.
           Living and eternal God, rule over us always.
           Amen.

or

Leader: Blessed are you, Sovereign God, source of light,
           giver of all things good!
           In your presence wisdom has prepared a feast;
           she calls the foolish to leave the ways of darkness;
           she welcomes us with truth and goodness.
           In Jesus your light has shone out;
           his cross has brought peace to the sinful.
           Your Spirit has opened our hearts;
           with all the saints we share your light.
           Refuge of the weary, hope of the dying,
           blessed are you, Sovereign God, light in the darkness.
           Amen.

           (John Melloh)

One of the following psalms may be said
           Psalm 18, 27, 43, 46, 92, 134, 136.1-9, 141,

Leader: May God, who gives us the light of his grace,
grant that we may come to behold
the light of his glory. **Amen.**

or

Eternal Light, shine into our hearts;
eternal Goodness, deliver us from evil;
eternal Power, be our support;
eternal Wisdom, scatter the darkness of our ignorance;
eternal Pity, have mercy on us;
that with all our heart and mind and strength
we may seek your face
and be brought by your infinite mercy
to your holy presence;
through Jesus Christ our Lord. **Amen.**

(Alcuin of York from "Prayers for use at the Alternative Services" © 1980 Mowbrays)

or   Yours is the day, O Lord, and yours is the night.
Let Christ the Sun of Righteousness abide in our hearts
to drive away the darkness of evil thoughts;
for he is our God for ever and ever. **Amen.**

(David Adam - "The Edge of Glory" SPCK/Triangle ©1985)

READING from the Bible *or other appropriate source*

e.g.   Genesis 1. 1-5   Let there be light
Deuteronomy 30. 11-20   Choose life
Isaiah 9. 2-7   The people that walked in darkness
Isaiah 49. 6b-13   A light to the nations
Isaiah 60. 1-6, 19   Your light has come
Luke 2. 29-32   A light to lighten the nations
John 3. 16-21   The Light of the world
John 8. 12-19   The Light of the world
Colossians 1. 13-20   Delivered from darkness
Revelation 22. 1-15   The Lord God will be their light

One of the following COLLECTS may be said

O Lord, you have given us your word
for a light to shine upon our path.
Grant us so to meditate on that word,
and to follow its teaching,
that we may find in it the light
that shines more and more until the perfect day;
through Jesus Christ our Lord.

O Lord,
you have set before us the great hope
that your kingdom shall come on earth,
and have taught us to pray for its coming:
give us grace to discern
the signs of its dawning,
and to work for the perfect day
when your will shall be done on earth
as it is in heaven;
through Jesus Christ our Lord.

(Percy Dearmer -
"Prayers for use at the Alternative Services" © 1980 Mowbrays)

Kindle, O Lord, in our hearts, we pray,
the flame of that love which never ceases,
that it may burn in us and give light to others.
May we shine for ever in your temple,
set on fire with that eternal light of yours
which puts to flight the darkness of this world
in the name of Jesus Christ your Son our Lord.

(St Columba)

Father of mercy,
continue we pray, your loving kindness to us all.
May we walk in the way of righteousness before you,
loyal to your law and clinging to good deeds.
Keep far from us all manner of shame, grief and care,
and grant that peace light and joy
may ever abide in our home(s);
for with you is the fountain of life,
and in your light we see light.

(from a Jewish eve of Sabbath devotion)

Be present, Spirit of God, within us,
your dwelling place our home;
may our darkness be dispelled by your light,
our troubles calmed by your peace,
all evil redeemed by your love,
all pain transformed in the suffering of Christ,
and all dying glorified in his risen life.

(Jim Cotter 1988 Cairn Publications, Sheffield)

The Service of Light ends with these words

Leader: Let us bless the living God
               He was born of the Virgin Mary,
ALL: **Revealed in his glory**
Leader: Worshipped by angels
ALL: **Proclaimed among the nations**
Leader: Believed in throughout the world,
ALL: **Exalted to the highest heavens.**
Leader: Blessed be God, our strength and salvation
ALL: **Now and for ever. Amen**

Hymns and Songs of Light

All earth was dark   MP 8

Brightest and best of the sons   AMNS 47, NEH 49, MP 69

Colours of day dawn into the mind   Come & Praise 54, JP 28

Christ whose glory fills the skies   AMNS 4, NEH 234, MP 79, CFW 134

Come Holy Ghost, our souls inspire   AMNS 448, NEH 138, MP 90

From the darkness came light   Come & Praise 29

God of mercy, God of grace   NEH 566, CFW 527

The ink is black   Come & Praise 67

Lead kindly light   AMNS 215, NEH 392, MP 399

The Light of Christ has come into the world   MP 652, CFW 8

Light of gladness, Lord of glory   CFW 154

Light of the minds that know him   NEH 400

Light up the fire   JP 28

Light's abode, celestial Salem   AMNS 185, NEH 54,

The Lord is my light, my light and salvation - Taize

Lord, the light of your love is shining (Shine Jesus shine)   MP 445

O for a closer walk with God   AMNS 231, NEH 414, MP 494

The people that in darkness sat   AMNS 52, NEH 57

The Spirit lives (Walk in the light)   MP 664

Thou whose almighty word   AMNS 180, NEH 466, MP 699

1: INTERCESSIONS with time for silence

This worship outline provides for long periods of quiet during which everyone can concentrate on the particular subject for which prayers are being offered, and if they wish say their prayers aloud. The Leader can then collect up all the prayers, both spoken and unspoken, by saying "Lord in your mercy". An appropriate verse of the Bible, or sentence, could be used at the beginning, or a quiet hymn or song could be sung.

Leader   Let us sit quietly for a while and draw away from all the busy things which have been occupying us, looking instead to our Father ....

Leader   Drop thy still dews of quietness
(or All)   Till all our strivings cease
                       Take from our souls the strain and stress
                           And let our ordered lives confess
                               The beauty of thy peace.

Leader   Oh Lord our Father, we come into your presence with awe; we thank you that we shall be received with love. **Amen.**

               (Time of quiet)

Leader   Your love and holiness remind us of our un-holiness.
               We acknowledge the times when we have made you sad
               by our actions and thoughts.
               We ask you to forgive us our times of laziness....
                       bad temper....   selfishness....
                       unkindness.....   impatience.....
                       disobedience....
               and other sins which we and you know about.....
               We ask in silence for your forgiveness.

(Time of quiet)

Leader   Grant, we beseech you merciful Lord, to your faithful people pardon and peace, that we may be cleansed from all our sins and serve you with a quiet mind; through Jesus Christ our Lord. **Amen.**
(Collect for 7 before Easter ASB)

Leader   We remember, God, with thanks the times recently when we have been very aware of your generosity to us.
We name them now .....

(Time of quiet)

Leader   Lord, in your mercy
All   **Hear our prayer**

Leader   Lord Jesus, we bring to you now, for your healing touch, those whom we know who are ill, at home or in hospital, and all who love and care for them.....

(Time of quiet)

Leader   Lord, in your mercy
ALL   **Hear our prayer**

Leader   We pray for those who are in trouble, or need of other kinds.....

(Time of quiet)

Leader   Lord, in your mercy
ALL   **Hear our prayer**

Leader   Father in heaven,
we, your children, bring before you our families,
and the children for whom we are responsible
as parents, godparents, or grandparents,
and as members of your Church in this place....

(Time of quiet)

Leader   Lord, in your mercy
ALL   **Hear our prayer**

Leader   Almighty God, we pray for the needs of this parish....

(Time of quiet)

Leader   Lord, in your mercy
ALL   **Hear our prayer**

Leader   Father of all,
we pray for the needs of the world,
and especially for peace and justice.....

(Time of quiet)

Leader   Lord, in your mercy
ALL   **Hear our prayer**

Leader   Finally we pray for the Mothers' Union here
and throughout the world, for family life
and for all who are married, as we say together

The Mothers' Union Prayer

Leader   O Lord, our loving Father,
we ask you to keep us, and those for whom we have prayed,
close to yourself,
that we may find in your love our strength and peace. **Amen.**

The Grace

(from Margaret Hopkins, Peterborough Diocese)

2: Prayers of PRAISE AND THANKSGIVING FOR THE LIVES OF WOMEN OF FAITH

CALL TO WORSHIP

Leader: Centuries of women are our sisters
ALL: **And we celebrate the lives they have lived**
Leader: We hold up half the sky
ALL: **And we see its beauty stretched out before us**
Leader: We have discovered the divine within us,
            around us and between us
ALL: **Let us celebrate this day and all that is before us**

Reading: Luke 1. 39-45 *(or other suitable passage)*

Pause for silent reflection

LITANY OF WOMEN THROUGH THE AGES

Leader: Holy Spirit of Life, we remember today the women, named
            and unnamed, who throughout time have used the power and
            the gifts you gave them to change the world. We call upon
            these, our forebears, to help us discover within ourselves
            your power, and the ways to use it to bring about the reign
            of justice and peace.

            We remember Sarah who with Abraham answered God's call
            to forsake their homeland and put their faith in a covenant
            with the Lord.
ALL: **We pray for her power of faith.**

Leader: We remember Esther and Deborah, who by acts of individual
            courage saved their nation.
ALL: **We pray for the power of their courage to act for the
            greater good**.

Leader: We remember Mary Magdalene and the other women who followed Jesus, who were not believed when they announced the resurrection.

ALL: We pray for the power of their belief in the face of scepticism.

Leader: We remember Phoebe, Priscilla, and the other women leaders of the early Church.

ALL: We pray for their power to spread the Gospel and inspire congregations.

Leader: We remember the abbesses of the Middle Ages who kept faith and knowledge alive.

ALL: We pray for the power of their leadership.

Leader: We remember St Teresa of Avila and St Catherine of Siena who challenged the corruption of the Church during the renaissance.

ALL: We pray for the power of their intelligence and their outspoken-ness.

Leader: We remember Florence Nightingale, Elizabeth Fry, Sophia Jex-Blake, Josephine Butler and all who worked to find justice for women in the Victorian era.

ALL: We pray for the power of their vision and their determination to change society.

Leader: We remember Mary Sumner who founded the Mothers' Union to be specially concerned for all that strengthens and builds up marriage and Christian family life.

ALL: We pray for the power of her courage and faithfulness.

Leader: We pray for our own mothers and grandmothers whose lives shaped ours.

ALL: We pray for the special power they attempted to pass on to us.

Leader: We pray for the women who are victims of violence in their own homes: may they be granted the power to overcome fear, and seek solutions.

ALL: We pray for those women who face a life of poverty and malnutrition: may they be granted the power of hopefulness to work together for a better life.

Leader: We pray for the women who are "firsts" in their fields: may they be granted the power to persevere and open up new possibilities for all women.

ALL: We pray for our daughters and granddaughters: may they be granted the power to seek that life which is uniquely theirs.

Leader: We have celebrated the power of many women past and present; it is time now to celebrate ourselves. Within each of us lie the seeds of power and glory. Our bodies can touch with love; our hearts can heal; our minds can seek out faith and truth and justice.

ALL: Spirit of life, be with us in our quest. Amen.

The Lord's Prayer

Blessing

Leader: Please turn to your neighbour and say
           "........., you too are blessed"
    or   "........., the peace of the Lord be with you" *and shake hands.*

Leader: May the blessing of the most holy Trinity:
           Creator - Redeemer - Sustainer
           keep us now and for evermore. **Amen.**

Where appropriate all may eat lunch or have other refreshments together.

(This service originated from the 1990 meeting of the Ecumenical Forum for European Christian Women in England. The Litany is adapted from words written by Ann M. Heidkamp)

3: ROUND THE YEAR

This outline order allows for the leader to include variable Bible Readings and prayers, appropriate to the day, season or chosen theme (see Chapter 13.4 and 5).

A seasonal or thematic introductory sentence may be used

Leader: O worship the Lord in the beauty of holiness
ALL: **Let the whole earth stand in awe of him**

Leader: God is Spirit
ALL: **They that worship him must worship him
in spirit and in truth.**

Leader: Through our weakness and ineffectiveness
we hinder the coming of God's kingdom.
Let us ask for pardon and forgiveness, saying together
ALL: **O most merciful Father,
we confess that we have done little
to forward your kingdom and to advance your glory.
Forgive our failures, pardon our shortcomings
and give us greater zeal in your service,
for Jesus Christ's sake. Amen.**

BIBLE READING *appropriate to the theme or season*
(see Chapter 13.4 or use other suitable reading)

THE COLLECT OF THE DAY
from the *Book of Common Prayer*, or the *Alternative Service Book*
(or one of the prayers from the seasonal selection Chapter 13.5)

INTERCESSIONS *led by the Leader, or others, or extempore,*
after each prayer these words may be sung

O Lord hear my prayer, O Lord hear my prayer,
When I call, answer me.
O Lord hear my prayer, O Lord hear my prayer,
Come and listen to me.

(© Ateliers et Presses de Taizé 71250 Taizé communaute, France)

A SEASONAL HYMN OR SONG *may be sung*

Leader: To end our time of prayer let us say together

The Lord's Prayer

The Mothers' Union Prayer

The Grace

1: COMMISSIONING OF OFFICERS

It is customary for officials to be commissioned in church during a diocesan, deanery or parish service appropriate to their area of responsibility. If the service is eucharistic the prayers for Mothering Sunday could be used and the special Post-Communion prayer.

Priest: We have come together here to worship God and to
(or Bishop) commission
            .... *(names, or e.g. "newly-elected members")* to office
            in the Mothers' Union; this is a joyful and important occasion.
            Each office carries great responsibility, for the Mothers'
            Union is a worldwide society within the Church, with special
            concern for all that strengthens and preserves marriage and
            Christian family life.

            ...., do you accept office in the Mothers' Union?

Answer: I do, the Lord being my helper.

Priest: Will you serve God in this way, in the firm belief that the
            power of the Holy Spirit will guide and direct all who call
            upon Him?

Answer: I will, putting my trust in him.

Priest *(taking each person in turn by the right hand):*
            ...., I admit you to the office of ....
            in the name of the Father, and of the Son
            and of the Holy Spirit. **Amen.**

When all have been commissioned the priest turns to the congregation and says:

People of .... ,
will you now welcome your new officer(s)?
and there can be a round of applause, or people can pass the peace.

Priest: will you remember .... in your prayers,
               and give her / them your loyal support and encouragement?

Congregation: We will

Priest: I call on you now to pray that God will bless his servant(s)
               and provide such gifts and powers as may be needed
               for the work ahead. Let us pray in silence ....

Priest: O God,
               we ask that you will bless your servants
               with a sense of your presence,
               and knowledge of your constant love.
               Give wisdom and understanding,
               your guidance and the humility to accept it.
               Grant all members the grace to support
               and uphold all who work in your name;
               through Jesus Christ our Lord. **Amen.**

               O God,
               you have called us from many nations and people;
               we ask you to bless the work of the Mothers' Union,
               and prosper its branches throughout the world.
               Give wisdom and courage to those who hold office
               and serve on its councils;
               unite its members in faith and love,
               and grant your peace in our hearts and homes,
               through Jesus Christ our Lord. **Amen.**

The Mothers' Union Prayer

A POST COMMUNION PRAYER *suitable for use if the commissioning takes place in a service of Holy Communion.*

Eternal God
by this Holy Sacrament you enable us to share in your love:
so bless us and all members of the Mothers' Union
that, being strengthened in love to you and to each other,
we may serve you faithfully to your glory,
through Jesus Christ our Lord. **Amen.**

*(Canon Frederick Ross, Vicar of Melbourne, Derbyshire
used with permission)*

2: ADMISSION / ENROLMENT OF NEW MEMBERS

The service of admission of new members should, whenever possible, take place in the context of regular Sunday worship. Where this is impossible, a deanery or other special occasion can be appropriate; if the admission is part of a branch meeting additional prayers, from which a selection can be made, are to be found in the blue service book.

The branch leader brings the candidate(s) forward, and any member(s) commended from elsewhere, to stand in front of the priest.

Priest: The Lord be with you.
ALL: **And also with you.**

Priest: We are now going to admit .... new members of the Mothers' Union, (and to welcome ... who have joined our branch).

The Aim of the Mothers' Union is the advancement of the Christian religion in the sphere of marriage and family life.

Leader: The Mothers' Union is a worldwide society within the Church. Its Objects are:
To uphold Christ's teaching on the nature of marriage and to promote its wider understanding;

To encourage parents to bring up their children in the faith and life of the Church;

To maintain a world-wide fellowship of Christians united in prayer, worship and service;

To promote conditions in society favourable to stable family life and the protection of children;

To help those whose family life has met with adversity.

The Purpose of the Mothers' Union is to be specially concerned with all that strengthens and preserves marriage and Christian family life. Membership is open to all who have been baptized in the name of the Holy Trinity.

Priest: ...., are you satisfied that these candidates have been adequately prepared for membership of the Mothers' Union?

Leader: I am.

Priest: To the best of your belief, do they understand the Aim, Purpose and Objects of the Mothers' Union, the commitment they are about to make, and the responsibility they will accept?

Leader: I believe they do.

Priest: *(to the candidate/s):*
             At your baptism you were signed with the sign of the cross to show that you must not be ashamed to confess the faith of Christ crucified. Do you stand by this?

Answer: I do.

Priest: We have just heard the Aim and five Objects of the Mothers' Union. Do you promise by God's grace to uphold and support them?

Answer: I do, the Lord being my helper.

Priest: Will you try to plan your life to include worship in church, prayer and Bible reading?

Answer: I will by the grace of God.

Priest   *(calling each person by name):*
             ...., I admit you to membership of the Mothers' Union in the name of the Father, and of the Son, and of the Holy

Spirit; *(handing a membership card to the new member)*
receive this card to remind you of your promises; and may
the Lord be with you.

(when all have been admitted)
Almighty God, Father, Son and Holy Spirit,
bless you and your home(s),
and your life and work for him,
and grant you the grace of perseverance to the end.

(to the congregation)
We have just witnessed the admission of .... (names) to
membership of the Mothers' Union. Will you do all you can to
welcome, support and pray for them?

ALL: **We will, in the name of the Lord.**

*If there are members who are joining from another branch, the priest
welcomes them by name, in these or other suitable words.*

Priest: .... we welcome you into the fellowship of this branch
of the Mothers' Union. May God bless you and your home(s),
and your work among us. **Amen.**

The Mothers' Union Prayer

*The service continues with the intercessions and/or the exchange of
the Peace.*

3: NEW BEGINNINGS - Opening a new group or branch

As the formation of a new branch is a parish occasion, the dedication should if possible take place at the main service on a Sunday in the parish church. It may include the commissioning of the branch chairman (p108), and the admission of new members (p111). Before the service the incumbent and members should meet to work out the aims for the new branch, and draft a Statement of Intent which sets these aims out clearly. It may reflect the Aim and Objects of the Mothers' Union or relate specifically to more local needs. If there is a new banner it can be dedicated.

The minister explains to the congregation the history of the formation of the new branch (group), and reads out the Aim and Objects of the Mothers' Union. The minister invites one of the members to read the Statement of Intent on behalf of the new branch.

Minister: May the Holy Spirit guide and strengthen you all,
             that in this, and in all things, you may do God's will
             in the service of the kingdom of Christ. **Amen.**

Minister: In the name of God I commend you to this work,
             and dedicate the branch to the glory of God.

             In the name of the parish of ....
             I pledge you our prayers, encouragement and support
             in the years ahead.

             Let us pray:
             Almighty God,
             look with favour upon this branch of the Mothers' Union;
             as the members reaffirm their commitment
             to follow Christ and to serve in his name,

give them courage, patience and vision;
strengthen them in their Christian vocation
of witness to the world, and service to others,
through Jesus Christ our Lord. **Amen.**

The Mothers' Union Prayer

One or more of the following prayers may be used as appropriate, or a hymn or song may be sung

Prayer of commitment *to be said by the members together*
**Heavenly Father,
As members of this branch we commit its life to you;
we seek your blessing in all we do:
your presence in our fellowship;
your inspiration in our activities;
your strength in our service to the Church
and to the community;
help us to be faithful in prayer and worship
and outgoing in our witness to the gospel,
that we may advance your kingdom,
and glorify your name,
through Jesus Christ our Lord. Amen.**

For the leader(s) of the group / branch
Everliving God, strengthen and sustain .... ,
that with patience and understanding
she may love and care for your people;
grant that under *her* leadership
the members of the branch may follow Jesus Christ,
offering to you their gifts and talents,
through him who lives and reigns with you
and the Holy Spirit,
one God, now and for ever. **Amen.**

For the branch

Lord we pray that our branch
may be like a house where people love to come:
may the way in be wide enough
for all who need human love and fellowship,
but narrow enough to keep out
all selfish ambition and petty jealousies,
all spite and narrow-mindedness.
Make the path smooth so that children may not trip,
nor the elderly or disabled stumble.
May the door be closed to the forces of evil,
but open to welcome the gifts of the Spirit.
May the windows let in the light of your presence,
and give us a vision of your kingdom;
we ask in the name of Jesus,
who welcomed old and young,
ate with publicans and sinners,
and gave his life for us. **Amen.**

For the dedication of a new banner

We dedicate this banner to the glory of God
in the name of the Father, and of the Son
and of the Holy Spirit.
May it be a symbol, visible to all who come to this church,
of our commitment to the advancement of the Christian
religion in the sphere of marriage and family life.
Father, we also dedicate ourselves,
as individuals and as a branch,
to serve you in following Jesus.
Help us to be faithful in worship, prayer and Bible reading,
and to help others to know your love.
We ask in the name of the same Jesus Christ, our Lord.
Amen.

For personal dedication *(where there is no banner)*

Father, we dedicate ourselves
to serve you faithfully and to follow Jesus,
to face the future with him,
seeking his special purpose for our lives.
Send us out to work and witness freely,
gratefully and full of hope,
in the power of the Holy Spirit,
and for the honour and glory of your Son,
Jesus Christ our Lord. **Amen.**

The Lord's Prayer

The Grace

and / or The Blessing

4: CLOSING A BRANCH OR GROUP

(These words can also be adapted to mark the end of a project)

It has been said that all good things must come to an end, but we often find it hard to face and accept when it is right to end an enterprise, or disband a group. Just as in a funeral an attempt is made to recognise the life and achievements of the person who has died, to offer comfort to those who are in mourning, and to affirm the eternal truth of Jesus as the Resurrection and the Life, so there are a number of similar aims in a service to mark the end of the life of a branch. It is also wise to recognise that among other feelings there may be guilt and regret for things done wrong or neglected.

Arranging this sort of service may be difficult if there are very few members left, but even if poorly attended, those who do come can be helped to value the past life of the branch, and to let go what might have been in the future, if only...

In accordance with the Constitution of the Mothers' Union a branch can only be closed after consultation with the Diocesan President and Secretary, and the observance of such other formalities as the Diocesan Constitution requires. Proper provision must be made for any remaining members to transfer to deanery or diocesan membership, and some mention may be made of their intention. The deanery Presiding Member should be invited. If possible some symbolic act should be performed e.g. the laying up of the banner, perhaps in a side chapel, or the packing up of official records to be handed over to the Diocesan Secretary.

The minister gathers the people together and explains informally the recent history of the branch and the reasons why it is appropriate to bring its existence to an end.

Minister: We have come together here to worship God and to thank him for what has been good in the past; this is an important but sad occasion, and we have mixed feelings, but we believe the right decision has been made.......

Listen to these words from the Bible:

"Think of the love that the Father has lavished on us, by letting us be called God's children; and that is what we are....

My dear people, we are already the children of God, but what we are to be in the future has not yet been revealed; all we know is, that when it is revealed we shall be like him because we shall see him as he really is." *(1 John 3. 1,2)*

This is the word of the Lord.

ALL: **Thanks be to God.**

The following prayers, or others, can be said by the minister or by members:

Thanksgiving for the past

Ever-loving Father,
we thank you for the work and witness
of the .... branch of the Mothers' Union:
for all by which it is remembered,
for all that it meant to those who belonged to it,
and those who were in any way helped by its members,
and for everything in its life
which reflected your mercy and love.
We pray for the members who have departed this life,
and for those who have moved away.
We recall the happy times in the past ....

For forgiveness

All-merciful Father
we bring to you for forgiveness all that was amiss
in the life of our branch over the years:
for failing to live up to your gospel:
for the things we were afraid to try,
and those we failed to finish;
for the times when we should have been reaching out
to your people in need but were turned in on ourselves;
for these and other shortcomings
we ask your forgiveness now. **Amen.**

Of hope for the future

We pray for the future of the remaining members:
that they may find comfort and fellowship elsewhere,
may remain true to their membership promises,
and may continue to know your love and power in their lives.

As we look forward we pray for the life of this parish:
that we may uphold Christ's teaching
on the nature of marriage
and help people to understand and follow it,
that children may be brought up
in the life and faith of the Church,
that family life be honoured and protected,
and that we may provide help
for all whose family life meets with adversity.
This we ask in the name of the same Jesus Christ our Lord.
Amen.

The General Thanksgiving *(said together)*

> Almighty God, Father of all mercies,
> we your unworthy servants
> give you most humble and hearty thanks
> for all your goodness and loving kindness.
> We thank you for our creation, preservation
> and all the blessings of this life;
> but above all for your immeasurable love
> in the redemption of the world
> by our Lord Jesus Christ,
> for the means of grace,
> and for the hope of glory.
> Give us, we pray,
> such a sense of all your mercies
> that our hearts may be unfeignedly thankful,
> and that we show forth your praise,
> not only with our lips but in our lives,
> by giving up ourselves to your service,
> and by walking before you
> in holiness and righteousness all our days;
> through Jesus Christ,
> to whom with you and the Holy Spirit,
> be all honour and glory, for ever and ever. Amen

(From the "Alternative Service Book " © 1980 The Central Board of Finance of the Church of England)

The Grace

5: AFFIRMATION OF MEMBERSHIP of the Church
and of the Mothers' Union

Minister: In the Decade of Evangelism we, the Church, have been called
to revitalize the proclamation of the Gospel, to re-dedicate our
lives to God, and to re-affirm the vows made at our baptism.
The Mothers' Union is a worldwide society within the Church
whose Objects are:

to uphold Christ's teaching on the nature of marriage and to
promote its wider understanding

to encourage parents to bring up their children in the faith and
life of the Church

to maintain a worldwide fellowship of Christians united in
prayer, worship and service

to promote conditions in society favourable to stable family life
and the protection of children

to help those whose family life has met with adversity.

The members of the Mothers' Union stand up before the minister

Minister: Members of the .... branch / deanery of the
Mothers' Union: at your admission as members you
re-affirmed the vows made at your baptism, and you
promised with the help of God to uphold and support the
Five Objects of the Mothers' Union. You also made a third
promise, to plan your life to include worship in church,
prayer, and Bible reading.
Having considered carefully the implications of these
promises, will you now re-affirm them?

Members: I re-affirm the vows made at my baptism and promise
            to uphold and support
            the Five Objects of the Mothers' Union by word and action,
            and to plan my life to include worship in church,
            prayer and Bible reading.

Minister: The Decade of Evangelism has called Christ's Church to
            make him known to the people of his world.

            As members of the Mothers' Union in the parish / deanery of
            ....,
            how do you propose to live out this call in your lives?

*The deanery / branch leader responds, reading out the resolve of the
branch / deanery.*

The Mothers' Union Prayer

RENEWAL OF VOWS

The Minister turns to the congregation and says
            Let us join with the Mothers' Union in a renewal of our
            baptismal vows:
All stand

Minister: I ask: do you turn to Christ?
ALL: **I turn to Christ**
Minister: Do you repent of your sins?
ALL: **I repent of my sins**
Minister   Do you renounce evil?
ALL: **I renounce evil.**

PROFESSION OF FAITH

Minister: I now ask you to make the profession of faith:
Do you believe and trust in God the Father,
who made the world?
ALL: **I believe and trust in him.**

Minister: Do you believe and trust in his Son, Jesus Christ,
who redeemed mankind?
ALL: **I believe and trust in him.**

Minister: Do you believe and trust in his Holy Spirit,
who gives life to the people of God?
ALL: **I believe and trust in him.**

Minister: This is the faith of the Church.
ALL: **This is our faith:**
We believe and trust in one God,
Father, Son and Holy Spirit. Amen.

ACT OF RE-COMMITMENT

Minister: Those who are baptized are called to worship and serve
God. From the beginning believers have continued in the
Apostles' teaching and fellowship, in the breaking of
bread in prayer.
Will you commit yourself to this life.
ALL: **I will, with the help of God.**

Minister: Will you forgive others as you are forgiven?
ALL: **I will, with the help of God.**

Minister: Will you seek to love your neighbour as yourself,
and strive for peace and justice?
ALL: **I will, with the help of God.**

Minister: Will you accept the cost of following Jesus Christ
in your daily life and work?
ALL: **I will, with the help of God.**

Minister: With the whole Church will you proclaim
by word and action the Good News of God in Christ?
ALL: **I will, with the help of God.**

**Heavenly Father,
through the power of the Holy Spirit,
renew our resolve to grow in faith
through prayer, Bible reading and worship.
Deepen and renew our love for you and for all people,
and give us the confidence
to share the good news of Jesus Christ with others.
We ask this in the name of him who calls us
to be his disciples. Amen.**

BLESSING

Minister: God bless you
(in the Decade of Evangelism and) in the years to come.
God prepare your hearts that you may be open
to his guidance, and the renewing influence of his Holy Spirit.
God revive, refresh and make you holy,
show each one of you what he would have you do,
as you follow Jesus, the Way the Truth and the Life.
May the love of the Lord Jesus draw you to himself,
the power of the Lord Jesus strengthen you in his service,
and the joy of the Lord Jesus fill your hearts;
and the blessing of God almighty,
the Father, the Son and the Holy Spirit
be among you and remain with you always.
ALL: **Amen**

1: FOR HEALING

Welcome and words of explanation about what is going to happen in the service and especially about the laying-on of hands.

OPENING RESPONSES

Leader: We come in this service to God
ALL: **In our need, and bringing with us the needs of the world**

Leader: We come to God, who has come to us in Jesus,
ALL: **And who walks with us the road of our world's suffering.**

Leader: We come with our faith and with our doubts;
ALL: **We come with our hopes and with our fears.**

Leader: We come as we are,
           because it is God who invites us to come.
ALL: **And God has promised never to turn us away.**

A song, hymn or psalm may be sung or said (see list)

A passage from the Bible may be read, one of the following, or some other
           Psalms 16, 23, 46, 103, 142
           Mark 1. 29-45, Mark 2. 1-12, Mark 9. 14-29,
           Luke 7. 18-29, Luke 11. 5-13, John 5. 1-15,
           John 14. 12-17, Acts 3. 1-16, 2 Corinthians 12. 7-10

PRAYERS OF INTERCESSION

One or more of the following may be used, followed by the names of people for whom healing is asked.

O Brother Jesus, you who walk with the wounded
along the road of our world's suffering,
we seek your grace of healing
for the broken people and places of our world:

O God, open to us today the sea of your mercy
and water us with full streams,
from the riches of your grace
and springs of your kindness.
Make us children of quietness and heirs of peace:
Kindle in us the fire of your love;
Sow in us your fear;
Strengthen our weakness by your power
And bind us closer to you and to each other

We bring to God someone whom we remember today,
and for whom we want to pray.....
We bring to God someone who is hurting today
and needs our prayer .....
We bring to God a troubled situation in our world today ...
We bring to God anyone whom we find hard
to forgive or trust...
We bring ourselves to God
that we might grow in generosity of spirit, clarity of mind,
and warmth of affection. **Amen.**

Leader: Jesus said "Come to me all you who are troubled
                 and I will give you rest"
                 So come,
                 you who are burdened by regrets and anxieties,
                 you who are broken in body or spirit,
                 you who are torn by relationships and by doubt,
                 you who feel deeply within yourselves
                 the divisions and injustices of our world.
                 Come,
                 for Jesus invites us to bring him all brokenness.

*Those who want to make special prayer either for themselves or for
someone else, or for the needs of the world, can be invited to come
forward, and kneel or stand while those who wish to share in the laying on
of hands may come and simply place a hand on the shoulder of the person
in front of them.*

*The Leader, alone or with others, or everyone, may use some of these or
other suitable words*
                 O great God, grant us your light.
                 O great God, grant us your grace.
                 O great God, grant us your joy
                 And let us be made pure in the well of your health.

                 Spirit of the living God, present with us here,
                 Enter you now, body, mind and spirit,
                 and heal you of all that harms you,
                 in Jesus' name. **Amen.**

                 God to enfold you.
                 Christ to touch you.
                 The Spirit to surround you. **Amen.**

May the healing touch of Jesus
the love of God the Father
and the power of the Holy Spirit
be upon you to cleanse, comfort and strengthen you
and to give you peace. **Amen.**

CLOSING PRAYER

Leader: And now may the God of hope fill us with all joy and peace in
believing, that we may abound in hope in the power of the
Holy Spirit. **Amen.**

*(This service is adapted from " A Service of Prayer for Healing" in the Iona Community
Worship Book, Copyright © 1991 The Iona Community Glasgow G51 3UU, Scotland,
reproduced by kind permission)*

Suggested songs, hymns and chants for a service of healing:

A brighter dawn   NEH 102

A stranger once did bless   AMNS 335

At even when the sun was set   NEH 243, MP 43

Be still and know   MP 48, JP 22

Be still for the presence of the Lord   MP 50

Bless the Lord, my soul - Taize

Bless the Lord, O my soul   MP 56

Father we adore you   MP 139

From thee all skill and science flow   AMNS 286

God be in my head   NEH 328

Jesu, Tawa Pano (Jesus, we are here) *"Many and Great"- songs of the World Church
Vol.1 (Wild Goose Publications, 1990)*

Just as I am   NEH 294, MP 396

Lay your hands gently upon us - Iona

Make way, make way for Christ the King   MP 457

Nada te turbe (Let nothing disturb you) - Taize

O for a thousand tongues   AMNS 125, NEH 415, MP 496

O God whose will is life   AMNS 408

O Lord hear my prayer - Taize

Peace, perfect peace   MP 555

Praise my soul, the King of heaven   NEH 436, CFW 459, MP 560

Spirit of the living God   MP 613

The Lord is my light - Taize

Thine arm O Lord, in days of old   AMNS 285, NEH 324

Thou to whom the sick and dying   NEH 325

Thou whose almighty word   AMNS 180, NEH 436, MP 560, CFW 459

Ubi Caritas et Amor (Where there is charity and love) - Taize

Veni, Sancte Spiritu - Taize

2: AT A TIME OF ADVERSITY

Leader: The Lord is near. Do not be anxious about anything, but in everything, by prayer and petition with thanksgiving, make your requests known to God. And the peace of God, which passes all understanding, will keep your hearts and minds in Christ Jesus. *(Philippians 4.5-7)*

A selection should be made from the following prayers, to suit the occasion and the people's concerns, with the addition of hymns or songs, Bible reading or other appropriate prayers (see references at the end).

The Love of God
Leader: What can separate us from the love of God?
             Can sickness or death?
ALL: **No nothing can separate us from the love of God.**

Leader: Can danger or war?
ALL: **No nothing can separate us from the love of God.**

Leader: Can sadness or despair?
ALL: **No nothing can separate us from the love of God.**

Leader: Can the nuclear bomb or the end of the world?
ALL: **No nothing can separate us from the love of God.**

Leader: Can failure or rejection?
ALL: **No nothing can separate us from the love of God.**

Leader: Can loneliness or fear?
ALL: **No nothing can separate us from the love of God.**

(David Adam from "The Edge of Glory" Triangle/SPCK Holy Trinity Church, Marylebone Rd. London NW1 4DU)

For God's will on earth

(if it is not possible for everyone to see a copy of the words, the leader can read both parts)

Leader: Let us ask God for the coming of his kingdom:

Leader: O God, into the pain of the tortured
ALL: **breathe stillness.**

Leader: Into the hunger of the very poor
ALL: **breathe fullness**

Leader: Into the wounds of our planet
ALL: **breathe well-being**

Leader: Into the deaths of your creatures
ALL: **breathe life**

Leader: Into those who long for you
ALL: **breathe yourself**

Leader: Your kingdom come, your will be done
ALL: **The kingdom, the power and the glory are yours, now and for ever. Amen**

(David Adam from "The Edge of Glory" Triangle/SPCK Holy Trinity Church, Marylebone Rd. London NW1 4DU)

For people in need *(as appropriate)*

Leader: We bring *(name)* in weakness
               For your strengthening

               We bring *(name)* in sickness
               For your healing

               We bring *(name)* in trouble
               For your calming

               We bring *(name)* in pain
               For your comfort

We bring *(name)* who is lost
For your guidance

We bring *(name)* who is lonely
For your love

We bring *(name)* who is dying
For your resurrection

Father us surround
every foe confound
      Jesus entwine
      keep us thine
Spirit enfold
in thy hold
      Sacred three enthrall
      to thee we call.

(David Adam from "The Edge of Glory" Triangle/SPCK Holy Trinity Church, Marylebone Rd. London NW1 4DU)

For people in prison

Merciful Father,
be with those in prison who have offended against the law;
may they come to know your love and forgiveness,
and turn to you in true repentance,
that they may have hope for the future
and the opportunity of making a fresh start.

Lord,
be with all political prisoners;
grant that they will not feel forgotten by the world at large;
give them courage and hope in their ordeal,
and help them according to their needs,
through Jesus Christ, our Lord. **Amen.**

(Freda Howes, Winchester Diocese "from Women at Prayer")

Prayer about war

Almighty and everlasting God, heavenly Father,
we thank you for your great love for us.
We pray you to change the hearts
of those who like their problems
to be solved in the way of war;
by killing innocent people all over the world
and making themselves glad
when destroying important places,
they have forgotten you.
Living God,
forgive them and send your Holy Spirit
to open their hearts and minds
so that if they carry their troubles to you
all can be solved in a peaceful way.
We pray you to save your innocent people
during this sad time, and protect them
through Christ our Lord. **Amen.**

(Yodita Elisa, Maridi Diocese, Sudan from "Women at Prayer")

Families in adversity

Despite our hopes and efforts, Lord,
we fail and things go wrong.
We offer you the mistakes we have made in ourselves
and in our marriages and families.
We pray for those who are suffering now
either from their own mistakes, or the mistakes of others:
for children separated from one parent,
and cut off from grandparents;
for parents who see their children for only part of the week;
for families who have many problems and lack hope;
for husbands and wives who no longer find joy in each other,
who feel wounded and disillusioned,

as their marriage breaks up;
for families who face death, illness or disablement
and feel they cannot cope;
for the unemployed who feel hopeless and unwanted.
We hold them before you Lord, for your healing love. **Amen.**
(Christine McMullen, MU "Anthology of Public Prayers")

O God, when we turn from you we fall
when we turn to you we rise,
when we stand with you we shall live for ever;
Grant us your help in all our duties,
your guidance in all our perplexities,
and your peace in all our sorrows,
through Jesus Christ our Lord. **Amen.**
(adapted from St Augustine of Hippo, 354-430)

Grant O God, your protection;
and in your protection, strength;
and in strength, understanding;
and in understanding, knowledge;
and in knowledge, the knowledge of justice;
and in the knowledge of justice, the love of it;
and in that love, the love of existence;
and in the love of all existence, the love of God,
God, and all goodness. **Amen.**
(Traditional Welsh prayer)

CLOSING WORDS:

> The Lord is faithful to all his promises
> and loving towards all he has made.
> The Lord upholds all those who fall
> and lifts up all who are bowed down...
> The Lord is near to all who call upon him,
> to all who call on him in truth.
> He fulfils the desires of those who fear him;
> he hears their cry and saves them.
> *(from Psalm 145)*

The Grace

(For prayers about family life see also chapters 8 and 9, and for other specific topics see also the "Mothers' Union Service and Prayer Books" and "Anthology of Public Prayers", and many other collections of prayers, including those mentioned in chapter 13.)

3: FOR RENEWAL

Leader: With great power the apostles gave their testimony to the
             resurrection of the Lord Jesus, and great grace was upon
             them. *(Acts 4. 33)*

Reading: Psalm 96 *(from Bible, Service or Prayer Book)*

*Pause for silent thought especially on the glory of God, his generosity to
his people, and our individual response (up to five minutes).*

PENITENCE:

Leader: Heavenly Father,
             we remember all the things which get in the way of doing
             your will: fear, busyness, complacency, defensiveness,
             apathy, failure, guilt:

             we are AFRAID of the demands which may be made upon us

             we are BUSY with tasks which help us feel useful,
             which nobody else will take on,
             which help our church run smoothly

             we are COMPLACENT because we have people in our church
             on Sundays, and as many children as we can manage

             we are DEFENSIVE about our past record,
             about the numbers in our congregation,
             about the size of our collection -
             people don't understand how difficult it is!

             we are ENERVATED by the apathy we know we shall meet,
             wearied by the look on people's faces when we ask for help

we are conscious of past FAILURE which makes us unwilling
to try anything ambitious or exciting

we are GUILTY of looking at ourselves,
rather than at you and at the people who need you

*Pause for silent thought, especially to discover what keeps each one of us
from telling people the good news of Jesus Christ*

Reading: John 20. 21-22

Leader: We pray for forgiveness,
               and ask that the Holy Spirit will come upon us
               dispel all our fears, and strengthen us:
               Lord in your mercy
ALL: **Hear our prayer**

Reading: Matthew 28. 16-end

Leader: We pray that we may be drawn to those who need you,
               that we may be able to make them your disciples
               and teach them your commands:
               Lord in your mercy
ALL: **Hear our prayer**

INTERCESSION

Leader: As Evelyn Underhill wrote
               "Real intercession is not merely a petition but a piece
               of work involving perfect, costly, self surrender to God
               for the work HE wants done on other souls"

               So Heavenly Father,
               we pray for renewal in the Church,
               we offer to you our own faith and love,
               and our readiness to hold to you, come what may;
               we offer our faith in the saving love of Jesus;

we offer our faith in the Holy Spirit,
present and active in the world,
in the hearts and minds of those
who do not yet recognise the love of Christ;
we offer ourselves as instruments of evangelism:
Lord in your mercy

ALL: **Hear our prayer**

Pause for silent or extempore prayer (say five minutes)

Leader: Heavenly Father
by his death and resurrection your Son, Jesus Christ
won the victory over sin and death, and set us free.
Grant us joy in believing now,
and grace both to rejoice with those who rejoice,
giving glory to you,
and to weep with those who weep,
sharing with them the good news
of your comforting presence,
and the hope of salvation through Jesus Christ our Lord.
Amen.

Almighty God,
you called your Church to witness
that you were in Christ
reconciling the world to yourself:
help us so to proclaim the good news of your love,
that all who hear it may be reconciled to you;
through him who died for us and rose again
and reigns with you and the Holy Spirit,
one God, now and for ever. **Amen**

(Collect for Pentecost 12 from the Alternative Service Book 1980,© The Central Board of Finance of the Church of England)

PART III

Resources

1: INTRODUCTIONS TO THE LORD'S PRAYER
to be said by the Leader

A: *(taken from "Celebrating Common Prayer")*

Sunday — Rejoicing in God's new creation, let us pray as our Redeemer taught us

As we come to the ending of the day let us pray as our Redeemer taught us

Monday — Being made one by the power of the Spirit let us pray as our Saviour has taught us

Tuesday — As we look for the coming of the Kingdom Lord teach us to pray

Wednesday — Rejoicing at the presence of God here among us, let us pray in faith and trust

Thursday — Let us pray for the unity of all peoples on earth in the words our Saviour has taught us

Friday — Lord Jesus, remember us in your Kingdom and teach us to pray

Saturday — As we await the fulfilment of the promise of his glory let us pray for the coming of the Kingdom

B: *(taken from the "Alternative Service Book")*
>As our Saviour Christ has taught us,
>we are bold to say

C: *(using words from the Mothers' Union Prayer)*
>United in prayer and worship, love and service,
>we say together the family prayer

D: *(Original)*
>Aware of our sisters and brothers worldwide,
>we pray in the words of Jesus, Saviour of us all,
>
>As children of the one heavenly Father,
>united throughout time and space
>we pray, as Jesus taught us
>
>We gather up all our prayers
>in the prayer Jesus gave his disciples

2: WORDS INVITING CONGREGATIONAL RESPONSES

A: *Greetings, to be used at the beginning of a service:*

Leader: The Lord be with you
ALL: **And also with you**

Leader: O Lord, open our lips
ALL: **And our mouth shall proclaim your praise**

B: *For the exchange of the Peace:*

Leader: The peace of the Lord be always with you
ALL: **And also with you**

C: *After a reading:*

Reader: This is the Word of the Lord
ALL: **Thanks be to God**

D: *In praise and thanksgiving:*

Leader: Lord of all creation
ALL: **We worship and adore you**
or
Leader: Father in heaven
ALL: **We give you thanks and praise**
or
Leader: Jesus, Son of God,
ALL: **We worship and adore you**
or
Leader: Jesus, Saviour of the world,
ALL: **We worship and adore you**
or
Leader: We are your people,
        we give you thanks and praise
ALL: **We praise your holy name**

E: *In intercession:*

Leader: Lord in your mercy
ALL: **Hear our prayer**

or

Leader: We pray to you, O God
ALL: **In faith we pray to you**

or

Leader: Jesus, Lord of Love (Lord of Life / Lord of the Church)
ALL: **In your mercy, hear us**

or

Leader: Father of all
ALL: **hear your children's prayer**

or

Leader: God of grace,
             accept our praise and thanksgiving
ALL: **and receive and grant our prayer**

or

Leader: Merciful Father
ALL: **accept these prayers**
             for the sake of your Son,
             our Saviour, Jesus Christ. Amen

F: *For confession:*

Leader:	Father forgive us
ALL:	**save us and help us**
or	
Leader:	Father in your mercy
ALL:	**forgive us and help us**
or	
Leader:	Lord have mercy
ALL:	**Christ have mercy**
Leader:	Lord have mercy
or	
Leader:	Lord, have mercy
ALL:	**Lord, have mercy**
Leader:	Christ, have mercy
ALL:	**Christ, have mercy**
Leader:	Lord, have mercy
ALL:	**Lord, have mercy**

G: *At the end of a service:*

Leader:	Go in peace to love and serve the Lord
ALL:	**In the name of Christ, Amen**
or	
Leader:	Go in the peace of Christ
ALL:	**thanks be to God**

3: HYMNS AND SONGS about family life

	AMNS	C&P	H&P	JP	MP	NEH
All creatures of our God	105	7	329		7	263
All the nations of the earth		14				
As your family, Lord			595			
At even when the sun was set	9		142		43	243
Bind us together, Lord				17	54	
Christ is made the sure foundation			485		73	205
Christ is our corner-stone	161					206
Colours of day		55		28		
Come down, O love divine	156		281		89	137
Eternal God, we consecrate	452					
Father God in heaven			518			
Father I place into your hands				42	133	
Father we adore you				44	139	
Father, who on man			341			
For I'm building a people				47	151	
For Mary, Mother of our Lord	360					161
For the beauty of the earth	104	11	333	48	152	285
God is here	464		653			
Happy are they, they that love	176		711			369
Happy the home			366			
Help us to help each other			374			
He's got the whole world		19	25	78	225	

	AMNS	C&P	H&P	JP	MP	NEH
How sweet the name of Jesus	122		257		251	374
Hushed was the evening hymn			523	85	253	
Immortal love for ever full	133		392		328	378
In Christ there is no east	376	66	758		329	480
Jesus calls us	312		141		359	200
Jesus Lord we pray	475		365			
Jesus shall reign	143		239		379	388
Join with us to sing		30				
Life is great, so sing	482					
Lord for the years					428	
Lord of all hopefulness	394	52	552	157		239
Lord of the home	494		367			
Lord you give to us			368			
Make me a channel of your peace			776	161	456	
May the grace of Christ	181		762			298
Now thank we all our God	205	38	566	175	486	413
O happy home			366			
Our Father, by whose name	505		371			
Our Father who art in heaven		51		192	661	
O God in heaven	407		369			
O love that wilt not let me go			685		515	
O perfect love	280		370		517	320

	AMNS	C&P	H&P	JP	MP	NEH
Tell out my soul	422		86	229	631	186
The Church of God a kingdom is	169					483
The Church's one foundation	170		515		640	484
The day thou gavest	16		648	236	641	252
The ink is black		67				
Think of a world		17	572	254		
We have a gospel	431		465		728	486
When I needed a neighbour	433	65		275		
When God made		16				
You, living Christ	533					487

KEY:

AMNS: Ancient & Modern New Standard pub. Hymns Ancient & Modern
C&P: Come & Praise pub. BBC Publications
H&P: Hymns & Psalms pub. Methodist Publishing House
JP: Junior Praise pub. Marshall Pickering
MP: Mission Praise (combined edition) pub. Marshall Pickering
NEH: New English Hymnal pub. The Canterbury Press

4: SUGGESTIONS for BIBLE READINGS ROUND THE YEAR

(many other suitable passages can be found, especially for Saints' days, in the lectionaries of the Church; it would be worthwhile to note your own ideas as well)

January

New Year	Joshua 1. 1-9, Romans 8. 28-29, 2 Corinthians 5. 17, Philippians 3. 13-14,
Epiphany	Matthew 2. 1-12, Matthew 3. 1-7, John 1. 29-34
Unity	John 17. 11b-23, 1 Corinthians 10. 17, Ephesians 2. 13-end, Ephesians 4. 1-6,
St Paul	Acts 9. 1-22, Acts 26. 15-18

February

Candlemas	Luke 2. 22-35
Lent	Psalm 51. 17, Daniel 9. 9, Matthew 6. 16-21, Luke 22. 28-30, Hebrews 4. 15-16

March

Women's World Day of Prayer	Matthew 6. 5-15
Annunciation	Matthew 1. 18-23, Luke 1. 26-38, Luke 1. 38, Luke 1. 46-49,
Mothering Sunday	Ruth 1. 8-17+22, Matthew 7. 21+24-27, Matthew 18. 1-6+10. Ephesians 5. 26-6. 4

April

Spring   Song of Songs 2. 10-13, Isaiah 61. 10-11

Eastertide   Matthew 28. 5- end, Luke 24. 13-35, John 20. 19,
              1 Corinthians 15. 3-11, 1 Corinthians 15. 12-20

St Mark   Mark 16. 15

May

Mary   Judith 13. 18-20, Luke 2. 19, Luke 2. 33-35+39-40,
              Luke 2. 51-2, Luke 11. 27-28, John 19. 25-27,
              Galatians 4. 1-5

Ascension   Mark 16. 14-end, Luke 24. 45-end,
              John 16. 12-15+25-end

Pentecost   John 15. 26-16. 7, John 16. 12-15, John 17. 1-11,
              Acts 2. 1-4, Acts 2. 1-11, Acts 2. 1-21, Acts 2. 32-42

The Church   Revelation 21. 1-5a

June

Trinity   John 3. 1-9, Revelation 4. 1-11

The Spirit   John 14. 23-26, 1 Corinthians 12. 4-13, Galatians 4. 6,
              Galatians 5. 16-25, Ephesians 5. 8-9

Baptism   Matthew 28. 18-end, Mark 1. 4-5+7-11, Mark 4. 1-11,
              Acts 8. 26-38

Petertide   Matthew 16. 13-20, Luke 9. 20

Ministry   Matthew 16. 24-27, Matthew 28. 16-end,
                     John 10. 11-16, John 20. 19-23, Romans 12. 1-13,
                     Romans 12. 14-16, 1 Corinthians 1. 21-end,
                     1 Corinthians 12. 4-13, Colossians 3. 12-17

July

Summer   Genesis 1. 31, Psalm 121, Song of Songs 2. 10-13

Holidays   Exodus 20. 9-11, Mark 6. 7-13 & 30-32

August

Mary Sumner   Luke 1. 38

September

Education   Proverbs 4. 1-9, Matthew 13. 52-end, John 16. 12-15,
                     1 Corinthians 2. 6-13

Holy Cross   John 12. 31-36a, 1 Corinthians 1. 18-23,
                     Galatians 6. 14, Philippians 2. 5-11

St Matthew   Matthew 9. 9-13

Harvest   Deuteronomy 28. 1-9, Psalm 24. 1, Psalm 104. 27,
                     Luke 13. 6-17, John 6. 22-40, 2 Corinthians 9. 6

Autumn   Genesis 1. 12

Angels   Psalm 103. 20, Acts 12. 6-11

October

One World   2 Corinthians 5. 14, Titus 2. 11

St Luke   Acts 1. 1, 2 Timothy 4. 5-13

The Church   Genesis 28. 17, Matthew 21. 12-16, John 10. 22-end

November

All Saints   Wisdom 3. 1-9, John 17. 24-26, 1 John 2. 15-17

Remembrance   Romans 8. 31b-end, 2 Corinthians 4. 7-end,
1 Thessalonians 4. 14, Revelation 21. 1-7

Mission   Matthew 9. 35-end, Matthew 28. 16-end,
2 Corinthians 4. 5, Colossians 1. 27

Winter   Genesis 8. 22, Psalm 135. 1-7

December

Advent   Luke 21. 36, Romans 13. 11

Christmas   Isaiah 9. 6, Luke 2. 10, John 1. 14, Titus 2. 11,
1 John 4. 9

St John   John 21. 20-end, John 21. 24

5: SUGGESTIONS FOR PRAYERS ROUND THE YEAR

(Suitable prayers for Saints' days can be found in the Prayer Book or Alternative Service Book).

New Year

I said to the man who stood at the gate of the year
"Give me a light that I may travel safely into the unknown".
And he replied:
"Go out into the darkness
and put your hand into the hand of God.
He will be better than any light
and safer than any known way".
So, God, we ask that we may know your presence with us,
take us by the hand and walk with us;
be for us the Way, the Truth and the Life
wherever we go this year;
we ask in the name of Jesus Christ.

(Anon.)

New Year

O God our Father,
at the beginning of this new year,
look upon our Christian family.
We bring to you our hopes and resolutions,
but also our doubts and fears.
Strengthen and inspire us for what lies ahead;
grant us courage and guidance
and the knowledge of your love for us,
that we may always live for you.

(Original)

Epiphany

O God, who by a star guided the wise men
to the worship of your Son;
we pray you to lead to yourself the
wise and great of every land,
that unto you every knee may bow,
and every thought be brought into captivity
through Jesus Christ our Lord. **Amen.**
*(Church in Jerusalem and the Middle East: from
the Anglican Communion "Prayers for the Decade"
reproduced with permission)*

Epiphany

Almighty God in Christ you make all things new;
transform the poverty of our nature
by the riches of your grace,
and in the renewal of our lives
make known your heavenly glory;
through Jesus Christ our Lord. **Amen.**
(Traditional)

Epiphany

Pour your light, Holy Spirit of God
into our hearts and minds.
Help us to know more clearly
and grasp more fully
the "Good News" of Jesus.
Help us then to know
how to share it with other people.
We ask this through Jesus Christ, who,
with you and the Father are One God. **Amen.**
(Diocese of Zululand, Southern Africa, from *the Anglican Communion*
"Prayers for the Decade", reprinted with permission)

Unity

Great God, you are one God,
and you bring together what is scattered
and mend what is broken.
Unite us with the scattered peoples of the earth
that we may be one family of your children.
Bind up all our wounds,
and heal us in spirit
that we may be renewed as disciples
of Jesus Christ, our Master and Saviour.

(from "Patterns for Worship"
©1989 The Central Board of Finance of the Church of England)

Unity

O God our Father,
unite your Church in one communion of disciples,
that together we may follow our Lord and Saviour
in all walks of life,
serving him together as instruments of mission in the world
and witnesses to His love in all nations
through Jesus Christ our Lord. **Amen.**

(Igreja Episcopal Anglicana do Brasil, from the Anglican Communion
"Prayers for the Decade", reprinted with permission)

Lent

God our Father,
in your love and goodness,
you have taught us to come close to you in penitence
with prayer, fasting and generosity;
accept our Lenten discipline,
and when we fall by our weakness,
raise us up by your unfailing mercy;
through Jesus Christ our Lord.

(David Silk - Mowbray 1980,
"Prayers for use at the Alternative Services" [altered])

Women's World Day of Prayer

Heavenly Father,
you call people of every race and every age,
every culture and every tradition,
to share in prayer and fellowship;
help us to become aware of the whole world,
to take up the burdens of other people,
and use our talents in the service of society,
always working to your honour and glory,
in the name of your Son, Jesus Christ,
and in the power of your Holy Spirit.

(original)

Mothering Sunday

God of compassion
whose Son, Jesus Christ, the child of Mary
shared the life of a home in Nazareth,
and on the cross drew the whole human family to himself;
strengthen us in our daily living
that in our joys and sorrows
we may know your presence to bind together and to heal;
through Jesus Christ our Lord,
who is alive and reigns with you and the Holy Spirit,
one God, now and for ever.

("Enriching the Christian Year" - Michael Perham)

Spring

We praise you, Lord, for this happy time of year,
when bud and blossom, blue sky and sunshine,
the song of birds and the scent of flowers
all remind us of your great love and goodness.
As the world of nature echoes your praise
may we join with the whole of creation
to worship your holy Name.

(Rowland Purton © 1973 in "Day by Day" pub Basil Blackwell)

Mary / Mothering Sunday

> May the love of the Holy Family surround us.
> May the joy that was Mary's refresh us.
> May the faithfulness that was Joseph's encourage us.
> May the peace of the Christ Child fill our lives.

Lady Day

> O Lord Jesus Christ
> give us, we pray, the graces of Mary:
> faith, patience, ready obedience, thankfulness and courage.
> As Mary said "My soul proclaims the greatness of the Lord,
> and my spirit rejoices in God my Saviour"
> so give us the gift of thankfulness and joy.
> As Mary "kept all these sayings in her heart"
> so may we be faithful in hearing and reflecting on your Word.
> As Mary said "Do whatever he tells you"
> grant us readiness to do the work to which we are called.
> As Mary stood by the cross
> grant that we may never be ashamed to confess you
> as our crucified and risen Saviour.

Easter

> God almighty
> we praise your holy name in this joyful Eastertide.
> We thank you, Lord,
> because through your death and resurrection
> we have won the victory and your redeeming grace and love.
> Loving Father God, fill us with new life
> so that we may love one another
> and do what you want us to do
> in sharing your love with those who do not know you;
> in Jesus' name we pray.
>
> *(Aipo Rongo Mothers' Union from the Anglican Communion "Prayers for the Decade" used with permission)*

The Holy Spirit

When I feel alone your presence is ever with me.
Come Holy Dove, cover with love

When I am in the dark your light is all around me
Come Holy Dove, cover with love.

When I am in the cold your warmth will enfold me
Come Holy Dove, cover with love.

When I feel weak your strength will seek me
Come Holy Dove, cover with love.

When I am sad your joy will make me glad.
Come Holy Dove, cover with love.

When I am sick and ill your health will heal me still.
Come Holy Dove, cover with love.

Spirit be about my head
Spirit peace around me shed
Spirit light about my way
Spirit guradian night and day
Come Holy Dove, cover with love.

(David Adam from "The Edge of Glory" ©Triangle/ SPCK)

The Holy Spirit

Father,
pour out your Spirit upon your people,
and grant to us:
a new vision of your glory;
a new faithfulness to your Word;
a new consecration to your service;
that your life may grow among us,
and your kingdom come;
through Jesus Christ our Lord.

(The Church in Australia - via the Anglican Communion "Prayers for the Decade" used with permission)

The Holy Spirit

God of power,
may the boldness of your Spirit transform us,
may the gentleness of your Spirit lead us,
may the gifts of your Spirit
equip us to serve and worship you
now and always.

(Original)

Baptism

Almighty and most merciful God,
the Father of our Lord Jesus Christ,
from whom every family in earth and heaven is named,
we praise and thank you
for adopting us as your children in Baptism,
for incorporating us in your holy Church,
and for promising that we are heirs in your kingdom.
Grant that we may be strengthened in our faith,
and filled with joy in knowing your love for us;
through the same Jesus Christ.

(Original)

Ministry

Almighty and everlasting God,
by whose Spirit the whole body of your faithful people
is governed and sanctified;
receive our prayers, which we offer before you,
for all members of your holy Church,
that each in their vocation and ministry
may truly and devoutly serve you;
through our Lord and Saviour Jesus Christ.

*(adapted from "The Alternative Service Book 1980"
© Central Board of Finance of the Church of England)*

Trinity

O Father, our hope:
O Son, our refuge;
O Holy Spirit, our protection;
O Holy Trinity: glory be to you.
(adapted from St Joanniki)

Summer

We thank you, Loving Father,
for the joys that summer brings:
for warm days and soft breezes,
for the trees and the flowers,
for the freedom to wear tee shirts and summer dresses,
for open doors and meals outside.
Help us to remember that all lovely things
come from you.
(Original)

Justice and Peace

Almighty Father we remember before you
those who have given their lives in the struggle for freedom,
and we pray that the justice and peace for which they fought
may be established today among the families of the nations;
we ask this in the name of him who taught us to pray
for the coming of the kingdom on earth as it is in heaven,
even Jesus Christ our Lord.
(Original)

Holidays

Almighty God, we thank you for the happiness of holidays,
and for the relaxation and refreshment they bring.
Watch over all who travel and keep them safe.
We pray for families on holiday at this time:
for children that they may be carefree
and enjoy new experiences, new places, new activities,

and for parents that they may be patient
and generous with their time and energy.
We pray for people who work to provide holidays for others.
Grant, Lord, that renewed and restored, your people
may return from holiday ready for the months ahead.
(Original)

Holidays

Father God, we thank you for our holidays;
for the excitement of preparing and packing to go away,
for interesting places to visit and explore
new people to meet and new customs to experience.
We pray for people who are unable to go away,
and for all who find holidays difficult.
Receive our prayer in the name of Jesus Christ
who gave us the example of taking time away.
(Original)

Education

Heavenly Father
we pray for all who are involved in education:
for teachers and lecturers,
that, as well as knowledge,
they may pass on a love of learning
for children and students, that they grow
in understanding and wonder,
for all whose work is to keep
schools and colleges running smoothly,
for those in government who plan and control education
that they may have sensible vision for the future.
Especially we pray for the people we know
who are involved in education ...
and for the work of education within the Church.
(Original)

The New School Year

O God our Father,
at the beginning of the school year (term),
we thank you for the holidays we have just enjoyed;
we ask for your blessing in the weeks ahead.
We pray for those who are starting school for the first time,
or going to a new school or course,
and for their families and friends who will miss them.
Help them all to work hard, find friends
and make the most of opportunities offered.
Bless all teachers and staff in schools and colleges;
we pray in the name of Jesus Christ
who spent three years teaching his disciples,
and blessed the children who came to him.   *(Original)*

Holy Cross

Almighty God,
whose beloved Son willingly endured
the agony and shame of the cross for our redemption;
give us courage to take up our cross and follow him,
who lives and reigns with you and the Holy Spirit,
one God, now and for ever.

(from the Book of Common Prayer
of the Episcopal Church of the United States of America)

Holy Cross

O Christ
who of your own will was lifted up on the Cross,
grant your mercies to the new community called by your name:
in your power make glad our hearts,
and give us victory over evil.
May we have for our help your armour of peace,
an invincible trophy.

(Kontakion for 14th September, from "A Manual of Eastern Orthodox
Prayers", adapted by Revd Ian Randall)

Harvest

Creator God,
you give seed for us to sow,
and bread for us to eat;
make us thankful for what we receive,
and do in us those generous things
that supply your people's needs;
so all the world may give you thanks and glory,
in Jesus Christ our Lord.

(This copyright material is taken from "A New Zealand Prayer Book –
He Karakia Mihinare o Aotearoa" (1989) and is used with permission)

Autumn

We praise you, God, for the joys of autumn:
for ripe fruit in the garden,
for the colours of the falling leaves,
for golden corn and scarlet berries.
As the days get shorter, and the evenings darker,
we pray for those who dread the coming of winter,
that they may stay well and warm until the spring.
We pray for all who look after the old and the young.
We ask in the name of Jesus, who, on the cross,
entrusted his mother to the care of the disciple John.

(Anon.)

Autumn

Almighty God,
you have blessed the earth and made it fruitful,
and have commanded us to work and share our bread,
bless our labours, bless our harvest;
help us to share the good things we enjoy,
and to make provision for all who are in need,
through Jesus Christ, our Lord.

(Original)

Angels

Blessing and honour,
thanksgiving and praise,
more than we can conceive,
more than we can utter,
be yours, most holy and glorious God
from all angels, all creatures, all people
now and for ever.

(Traditional)

Angels

Everlasting God,
you have ordained and constituted
in a wonderful order the ministries of angels and mortals:
mercifully grant that,
as your holy angels always serve and worship you in heaven,
so by your appointment
they may help and defend us here on earth;
through Jesus Christ, our Lord.

(from the Book of Common Prayer of the Episcopal Church of the United States of America)

One World

God of revelation,
whose mercy embraces all people and all nations:
tear down the walls that divide us,
break open the prisons which hold us captive
and so free us
to celebrate your beauty in all the earth;
through Jesus, our Brother and our Redeemer.

(from "Celebrating Common Prayer" ©1992 The European Province of the Society of Saint Francis)

Luke / Healing

Lord God of heaven,
you gave your servant Luke skill as a doctor,
a sympathetic understanding of people in need,
and loyalty to his friends in trouble and in prison;
we pray for those who need healing and understanding,
support and friendship today ....
we pray for ourselves,
and for all who try to help others,
that we may learn patience and wisdom,
and give ourselves fully in your name,
through Jesus Christ our Lord.

(original)

The Church

Almighty God,
you have built your Church
upon the foundation of prophets and apostles,
with Jesus Christ himself as the chief corner-stone;
join us together, in unity of spirit,
that we may become a holy temple, acceptable to you,
through the same Jesus Christ our Lord.

(original)

Peace and Remembrance

God, the God of eternal peace,
whose reward is the gift of peace,
and whose children are the peacemakers;
pour your peace into our hearts
that conflict and discord may vanish,
and our love and desire be always for your peace,
through Jesus Christ our Lord.

(Mozarabic)

Mission

Eternal Giver of love and power,
your Son, Jesus Christ, has sent us into all the world
to preach the gospel of his kingdom.
Confirm us in this mission,
and help us to live the good news we proclaim;
through the same Jesus Christ our Lord.

("Enriching the Christian Year" - Canadian Book of Alternative Services)

Mission

Almighty God give us your Holy Spirit
so that we may have power to speak about you,
and not be afraid to spread your Word throughout the world.
May we ourselves show the world your Word
through our actions
and know that you are always with us,
through Jesus Christ our Lord.

*(from the Church of Melanesia -
via "Prayers for the Decade" from the Anglican Communion)
reproduced with permission)*

Winter

Heavenly Father we thank you for the joys of winter:
for the beauty of snow and frost, for rain to water the earth,
for warm clothes and the security of our homes,
for indoor activities
and (preparations for Christmas) / (the promise of spring).
We pray for those who are unhappy in winter
or at Christmas; help us to help them.

(original)

6: STANDARD TEXTS of frequently used prayers

(see also inside and back of cover)

Mary Sumner's Personal Prayer

All this day, O Lord,
let me touch as many lives as possible for thee;
and every life I touch,
do thou by thy Spirit quicken,
whether through the word I speak,
the prayer I breathe, or the life I live.

(As this is Mary Sumner's prayer it is included unmodernised)

The Magnificat - modern

My soul proclaims the greatness of the Lord:
    my spirit rejoices in God my saviour;
for he has looked with favour on his lowly servant:
    from this day all generations will call me blessed.
the Almighty has done great things for me:
    and holy is his name.
He has mercy on those who fear him:
    in every generation.
He has shown the strength of his arm:
    he has scattered the proud in their conceit.
He has cast down the mighty from their thrones:
    and has lifted up the lowly.
He has filled the hungry with good things:
    and the rich he has sent away empty.
He has come to the help of his servant Israel:
    for he has remembered his promise of mercy,
the promise he made to our fathers:
    to Abraham and his children for ever.
Glory to..

The Magnificat - traditional

My soul doth magnify the Lord:
   and my spirit hath rejoiced in God my Saviour.
For he hath regarded:
   the lowliness of his handmaiden.
For behold, from henceforth:
   all generations shall call me blessed.
For he that is mighty hath magnified me:
   and holy is his name.
And his mercy is on them that fear him:
   throughout all generations.
He hath shewed strength with his arm:
   he hath scattered the proud
   in the imagination of their hearts.
He hath put down the mighty from their seat:
   and hath exalted the humble and meek.
He hath filled the hungry with good things:
   and the rich he hath sent empty away.
He remembering his mercy hath helpen his servant Israel:
   as he promised to our forefathers,
Abraham and his seed, for ever.
Glory be..

The Nunc Dimittis

Lord now you let your servant depart in peace:
   your word has been fulfilled.
My own eyes have seen the salvation:
   which you have prepared in the sight on every people;
a light to reveal you to the nations:
   and the glory of your people Israel.
Glory to ..

SOME BOOKS with more WORDS FOR WORSHIP

David Adam : *The Edge of Glory, Tides and Seasons, Border Lands, Power Lines* (S.P.C.K. / Triangle)

George Appleton : *Daily Prayer and Praise* (Lutterworth)

Michael Botting : *For All The Family, More For All The Family, Drama For All The Family etc.* (Kingsway)

Tony Castle : *A Treasury of Prayer* (Hodder & Stoughton)

Frank Colquhoun : *New Parish Prayer, Contemporary Parish Prayers, More Parish Prayers, Family Prayers etc.* (Hodder & Stoughton)

Alan Gaunt : *New Prayers for Worship* (John Paul, the Preachers Press)

Kahlil Gibran : *The Prophet* for helpful material about Marriage, Parents and Children, Love, and Work. (Heinemann)

Giles and Melville Harcourt : *Short Prayers for the Long Day* (HarperCollins)

Donald Hilton: *Words to Share, Liturgy of Life* (N.C.E.C)

Paul Iles: *The Pleasure of His Company* (Kevin Mayhew)

The Mothers' Union : *Anthology of Public Prayers, The Mothers' Union Prayer Book, The Mothers' Union Service book*

J.M.Mountney : *Songs and Prayers of the Church* contains useful canticles (Mowbrays)

New Every Morning, prayers from the BBC's Daily Service (B.B.C.)

Michael Perry : *Bible Praying* (Fount), *The Dramatised Bible*
(Marshall Pickering / The Bible Society),
Church Family Worship (Hodder)

Susan Sayers : *Springboard to Worship* especially for litanies and forms
of intercession and *Intercessions for the Christian Year*
(Kevin Mayhew Ltd)

David Silk : *Prayers for Use at Alternative Services* (Mowbrays)

The Society of St Francis : *Celebrating Common Prayer* particularly
Bible canticles, and psalm prayers

Rachel Stowe : *Women at Prayer* (Marshall Pickering)

HYMN BOOKS

Ancient & Modern New Standard
Hymns Ancient & Modern, St Mary's Works, St Mary's Plain,
Norwich,Norfolk NR3 3BH

Come & Praise
British Broadcasting Corporation, 35 Marylebone High Street,
London W1M 4AA

Hymns & Psalms
Methodist Publishing House, 20 Ivatt Way, Peterborough, Cambs, PE3 7PG

Junior Praise
published by Marshall Pickering, an imprint of HarperCollins Publishers
77-65 Fulham Palace Road, Hammersmith, London W6 8JB

Mission Praise (combined edition)
published by Marshall Pickering, an imprint of HarperCollins Publishers
77-65 Fulham Palace Road, Hammersmith, London W6 8JB

New English Hymnal
The Canterbury Press, St Mary's Works, St Mary's Plain, Norwich,
Norfolk NR3 3BH

USEFUL ADDRESSES

Ateliers et Presses de Taizé, 71250, Taizé communaute, France
produce books and cassettes of scriptural chants; permission is always
needed for reproduction.

**The Central Board of Finance of the Church of England, Church
House, Great Smith Street, London SW1P 3NZ** *Patterns for Worship,
The Promise of His Glory,* and *The Alternative Service Book 1980.*

**Christian Aid, Inter-Church House, 35-41 Lower Marsh, London
SE1 7RL** produces very useful material for Harvest, Advent and One-World
Week with a worldwide angle on worship.

**Church House Publishing, Church House, Great Smith Street,
London SW1P 3NZ** *Flowers, Fonts and Fuzzies, Our Mum,* and
Together magazine which contains useful material and advice about
worship with children.

**Church Pastoral Aid Society, Athena Drive, Tachbrook Park,
Warwick CV34 6NG** produces material for worship and support for
women's groups.

FLAME, 11 Mundy Street, Heanor, Derbs. DE7 7EB has produced
useful worship material on family themes, especially for the International
Year of the Family (1994).

**The Secretary for Liturgy SSF, Hillfield Priory, Dorchester, Dorset,
DT2 7BE,** administers the copyright for *Celebrating Common Prayer*
©1992 The European Province of the Society of St Francis.

The Iona Community, Pearce Institute, 840 Govan Road, Glasgow, G51 3UU *Iona Community Worship Book, The Wee Worship Book,* and several books and cassettes of collections of songs and books of sketches and prayers. Iona are most generous in allowing free reproduction for one-off usage; see instructions in most of their publications.

Jubilate Hymns Ltd, 61 Chessel Avenue, Southampton, Hants SO19 4DY *Church Family Worship;* they also own the copyright of many modern worship songs.

Kingsway Publications Ltd, 1 St Anne's Road, Eastbourne, East Sussex, BN21 3UN publish *For all the Family* and *More for all the Family,* books of material for family services edited by Michael Botting.

A.R. Mowbray Ltd., Artillery House, Artillery Row, London SW1P 1RT *Prayers for Use at Alternative Services* ©1980 Mowbrays

SPCK Triangle Holy Trinity Church, Marylebone Road, London NW1 4DU publishers of *Enriching the Christian Year* and *The Edge of Glory etc.* by David Adam

The Lord's Prayer *(see chapter 13.1 for words of introduction)*
Our Father in heaven,
hallowed be your name,
your kingdom come,
your will be done,
on earth as in heaven.
Give us today our daily bread.
Forgive us our sins
as we forgive those who sin against us.
Lead us not into temptation
but deliver us from evil.

For the kingdom, the power,
and the glory are yours
now and for ever. **Amen.**

The Lord's Prayer - *traditional*
Our Father, who art in heaven,
hallowed be thy name;
thy kingdom come;
thy will be done;
on earth as it is in heaven.
Give us this day our daily bread.
And forgive us our trespasses,
as we forgive those who trespass against us.
And lead us not into temptation;
but deliver us from evil.

For thine is the kingdom, the power, and the glory,
for ever and ever. **Amen.**

(Extracts from "The Book of Common Prayer", the rights in which are vested in the Crown, are reproduced by permission of the Crown's Patentee, Cambridge University Press)